Launching Your

Business

Frank Fiore
Linh Tang

D1560522

800 East 96th Street,
Indianapolis, Indiana 46240

Launching Your Yahoo! Business

International Standard Book Number: 0-7897-3533-4

Library of Congress Catalog Card Number: 2006920305

Printed in the United States of America

First Printing: March 2006

09 08 07 06   4 3 2

Trademarks

Warning and Disclaimer

Bulk Sales

Que Publishing offers excellent discounts on this book when ordered in quantity for bulk purchases or special sales. For more information, please contact

U.S. Corporate and Government Sales
1-800-382-3419
corpsales@pearsontechgroup.com

For sales outside the United States, please contact

International Sales
international@pearsoned.com

Associate Publisher
Greg Wiegand

Acquisitions Editor
Stephanie J. McComb

Development Editor
Kevin Howard

Managing Editor
Charlotte Clapp

Project Editor
Andy Beaster

Indexer
Ken Johnson

Technical Editor
Lon S. Safko

Publishing Coordinator
Sharry Lee Gregory

Interior Designer
Anne Jones

Cover Designer
Anne Jones

Page Layout
Susan Geiselman

Contents at a Glance

Table of Contents

Part IV: Launching Your Yahoo! Store

Part V: Managing Day-to-Day Business

About the Authors

Frank Fiore is an acknowledged eBusiness expert and accomplished author of six eBusiness books that have sold more than 50,000 copies: *The 2005 Online Shopping Directory for Dummies, Successful Affiliate Marketing for Merchants, e-Marketing Strategies, The Complete Idiot's Guide to Starting an Online Business, Dr. Livingston's Online Shopping Safari Guidebook, TechTV's Starting an Online Business,* and *How to Succeed in Sales Using Today's Technology.* His most recent book from Que Publishing is *Writing a Business Plan In No Time.* He was the online shopping guide for About.com and is a prolific writer of eBusiness features on Informit.com. In addition to his writing endeavors, he has appeared on numerous TV and radio talk shows discussing online shopping and the future of eCommerce, and he teaches college-level courses on eBusiness at Western International University. He lives in Paradise Valley, Arizona, with his wife and their Scottish sheepdog.

Linh Tang is an award-winning web designer, certified search engine optimizer, and eMarketing expert. Linh has been designing websites since 1995 and developing Yahoo! stores since 2000. He is the founder of Beyond Ideas, LLC, an Internet development and marketing consulting company, and cofounder of Paper Models Inc., both based in San Diego, California. Some of his clients include Fortune 100 companies and government organizations. He has a proven track record of increasing companies' web traffic and online sales. He lives in San Diego, California, with his wife and son.

Dedication

To my son Christopher, who is just entering the world of eCommerce. Good luck with your new endeavor. —F.F.

*To my son Tristan, "You're my sunshine, my only sunshine, you make me happy...."
A very special thank you to my wife, Cathy: I wouldn't be where
I am today without you. To my friends and family, especially my mom, thank you for your encouragements on this venture. Lastly, to my friend and business partner, Lon Safko, thank you for your support. This is only the
beginning. —L.T.*

Acknowledgments

We would like to acknowledge two very special people who helped make this book a success: Paul Boisvert, senior technical content producer at Yahoo!, for reviewing the manuscript for Yahoo! store accuracy; and Lon Safko, technical editor at Que Publishing. Thanks guys, you were a great help in keeping us on the technical straight and narrow. A special thanks to Stephanie McComb, our acquisitions editor at Que, who believed in this project and who saw to it that it got to see the light of day, and Kevin Howard, whose help was invaluable in developing the book for sale.

We Want to Hear from You!

As the reader of this book, *you* are our most important critic and commentator. We value your opinion and want to know what we're doing right, what we could do better, what areas you'd like to see us publish in, and any other words of wisdom you're willing to pass our way.

As an associate publisher for Que Publishing, I welcome your comments. You can email or write me directly to let me know what you did or didn't like about this book—as well as what we can do to make our books better.

Please note that I cannot help you with technical problems related to the topic of this book. We do have a User Services group, however, where I will forward specific technical questions related to the book.

When you write, please be sure to include this book's title and author as well as your name, email address, and phone number. I will carefully review your comments and share them with the author and editors who worked on the book.

Email: feedback@quepublishing.com

Mail: Greg Wiegand
         Associate Publisher
         Que Publishing
         800 East 96th Street
         Indianapolis, IN 46240 USA

For more information about this book or another Que title, visit our website at www.quepublishing.com. Type the ISBN (excluding hyphens) or the title of a book in the Search field to find the page you're looking for.

If you've spent any time watching infomercials on TV or have an email account, you most likely ran across someone or some company trying to sell you on the idea of starting an online business. All you had to do was buy their Internet money-making package. It was yours for the asking. They were asking $79.95, paid out in three equal installments. You might also have heard the testimonials and how you can make money selling just about anything you could think of on the Internet.

And doing this while you slept!

If you haven't found out by now, making money by opening a business on the Internet is not easy. To paraphrase the famous twentieth century actor Edmund Gween's deathbed quote, "Dying is easy—eCommerce is hard." Looking at the littered landscape of failed eCommerce sites after the dotcom bust, one would believe that to make a small fortune in eCommerce, one would have to start with a large one.

If you want to set up your own online business or extend the one you have, and have dreams of becoming the next Amazon, there's both good news and bad news in the eCommerce world of today.

First the bad news.

Why is it so difficult to build a successful online business? Well, there are a variety of reasons and they come in all sizes—small, medium, and large. There's the small cost of maintaining a full-blown eCommerce site. You need a web server—that is, someplace to host your eCommerce website. Then you have the medium cost of receiving and sending emails, taking orders online, processing credit cards, and not to mention the high cost of a host of software applications and the programmers to use them to build and maintain your online storefront. And all this reaches deep into your pocket even before you ship your first order or provide your first service. And you better have deep pockets because establishing and maintaining an online storefront can run into the thousands of dollars.

Now, the good news.

There is a light at the end of this gloomy tunnel of expenses. And it has a name: Yahoo! store. It's been a mere 10 years since the appearance of the first eCommerce site on the Net. Since then, a lot of digital river has run under the eCommerce bridge, but one thing is certain. eCommerce is here to stay. One case in point is the Yahoo! stores. All through the eCommerce turbulence and dot-com bust, the Yahoo! network of stores has grown and is growing stronger.

If you are an individual who wishes to dip his or her toe into the eCommerce river, and want to set up a part-time home business, then establishing a Yahoo! store could fill the bill—and fill it for what you might pay for video rentals for a month. You can set up a Yahoo! store for as little as $39.95 a month, a small fee per transaction of 1.5%, plus a $50 setup fee. To add icing on the cake, a simple store can be created in 24 working hours using nothing but your web browser.

The Yahoo! stores have grown into one of the largest online shopping destinations on the Web today. The Kelsey Group estimates that approximately 20% of U.S. websites are eCommerce enabled and that there are a total of approximately 300,000 eCommerce websites currently operating in the U.S. market. Based on the number of eCommerce stores (300K) and the number of Yahoo! hosted online stores (almost 40K), nearly 40,000 merchants currently use Yahoo! Small Business solutions for their eCommerce needs. That is, Yahoo! hosts approximately 1 out of 8 online stores.

Now that's a strong business partner!

So why is Yahoo! store so popular? Because of what it offers for the asking price. Speed and ease of setting up your store. A comparatively small fee that covers all software costs, secure site hosting, traffic and sales tracking, a payment gateway to process credit cards with your merchant account, 24-hour toll-free phone support, regular website backups and restores, valuable marketing tools for your store, and importantly, exposure on Yahoo! Shopping, one of the most frequented eCommerce destination on the Net.

The end result of this bargain storefront technology is a huge interest by businesses to take the eCommerce plunge with a Yahoo! store, because a part-time home business can save thousands of dollars in programming costs, without the need of any technical skills whatsoever. You might think that because of its price, a Yahoo! store is an amateurish, meagerly featured, dumbed-down version of a real online storefront.

Not so.

For the economical price, you will get a full-featured online storefront built for professional eCommerce. But don't take our word for it. There are more online storefronts built with Yahoo! store than any other online store software. Big names such as Ben & Jerry's, NASA, the Guggenheim Museum, Pepsi Cola, and Yosemite National Park are just a few of the big companies and organizations that have trusted Yahoo! store for their eCommerce solution.

With Yahoo! store, there is simply no easier way to have a high-quality, professional-looking, secure online store.

Who Should Buy This Book

If you have a product, service, or hobby, or just want to prove out a business idea and would like to test it out with little risk or cost to you, and are looking for a way to create an online presence without the need of programming or design skills, then *Launching Your Yahoo! Business* will show you how by using the resources and technology of the Yahoo! store. Yahoo does provide a booklet with instructions on how to build and launch a Yahoo! store, but it is limited. *Launching Your Yahoo! Business* includes that information but goes much further by offering tips and proprietary instructions on building your Yahoo! store quickly and with little hassle, in addition to showing you how, using a Yahoo! store, you can benefit from Yahoo!'s extensive reach and leverage of the Yahoo! Shopping Network to access potential customers.

Once you have successfully launched your part-time home business, our second book, *Succeeding at Your Yahoo! Business*, will help you grow that acorn of a business into a full-time business.

What's in This Book

Launching Your Yahoo! Business will give the part-time home business owner an overview of eCommerce and what it is, what makes up an eCommerce website, and how a Yahoo! store can be used to bring a business idea online, without confusing technical jargon or minute details that will tend to confuse the new Yahoo! store user that other books on the Yahoo! store program tend to be. Our intent is not to overload you with information, but to show you how easy it is to open a credible and effective basic Yahoo! store that will put you in business within a few days. This book will help you choose the right way to develop a Yahoo! store for your online business, learn the basic elements of a business plan, and discover how easy and fast it is to set up and launch a Yahoo! store, including basic marketing strategies and managing a Yahoo! store's day-to-day business.

Sidebars

In addition to the basic information in the text, *Launching Your Yahoo! Business* includes several sidebars that include a definition of terms, tips, warnings, and directions to web resources.

The **Yahoo! Talk** sidebar describes the different terms Yahoo uses when describing its store technology and procedures. Understanding these terms will help you better comprehend the instructions and concepts in the text.

The **Warning** sidebar alerts you to possible mistakes you may make when setting up and launching your Yahoo! store. By avoiding these mistakes or misunderstandings, you will be able to establish your Yahoo! store without having to repeat steps or make time-consuming changes.

The **Tip** sidebars will help you set up, launch, and manage your Yahoo! store in a more efficient manner and help you save time and money.

The **Web Resource** sidebars will point your to valuable resources on the World Wide Web that will help you manage and market your Yahoo! store.

Finally, we have established a website at www.MyEcommerceSuccess.com to inform you of the latest developments in the Yahoo! store. The Net moves fast and to stay ahead of the game, you need to stay up-to-date not only on the new developments with Yahoo! store but also the newest developments in eCommerce. We suggest that you visit our website frequently. In addition, you will see throughout this book sidebars labeled **Free Informative Article** that offer free valuable articles on the My Ecommerce Success website for you to download once you register at the website. You can register by visiting www.MyEcommerceSuccess.com using the ISBN (0-7897-3533-4) of this book. Besides the free articles referenced in the **Free Informative Article** sidebars, we offer a periodic *eCommerce Management Newsletter* on managing and marketing your eCommerce storefront that will keep you abreast of the latest developments in eCommerce along with other valuable resources.

Yahoo! Store Setup Steps

Here's a handy step-by-step checklist on how to set up your Yahoo! store and where to find the instructions in the book. Keep it by your side when creating and maintaining your Yahoo! store.

Step 1: Register your domain name and sign up for a Yahoo! Merchant Solutions account.

- Registering your domain name: 58
- Selecting a Merchant Solutions package: 100

Step 2: Explore the Manage My Services control panel.

- Manage My Services control panel: 121

Step 3: Accept payments online. Sign up for a merchant account or use your existing merchant account.

- Setting up your merchant account: 148
- Signing up with Paymentech: 148
- Using your own merchant account: 148

Step 4: Organize and add products to your store.

- Adding products: 124
- Adding products with Store Editor: 125
- Adding products with Catalog Manager: 127

Step 5: Plan your storefront content and products.

- Organizing your materials: 118

Step 6: Customize your store layout and navigation.

- Customizing your store: 134

Step 7: Configure your backend systems and operations.

- Setting up shipping options: 140
- Setting up tax tables: 153
- Setting up order notifications: 155

Step 8: Develop your merchandising strategy.

- Developing your merchandising strategy: 188
- Cross-selling: 189
- Gift certificates: 190
- Coupons: 191

Step 9: Launch and market your storefront for business.

- Publish your store: 137
- Basic marketing—Promoting your Yahoo! store for free: 161
- Search engine optimization: 171

Step 10: Process and manage your orders.

- Process orders: 202
- Retrieve orders: 205
- Preventing fraudulent orders: 209

Step 11: Monitor site and sales statistics.

- Viewing site statistics: 215
- Viewing sales statistics: 218

Okay. Let's dive in and get to work!

Part I

Putting the "e" in Commerce

eCommerce Basics

By the end of the first decade of the twenty-first century, the eCommerce world on the Internet will contain tens of thousands, or more likely hundreds of thousands, of eCommerce websites, all competing for the attention and wallet of the online consumer. The vast majority of these eCommerce sites will be part-time or home businesses selling a limited number of products or services. Since you're reading this book, you've decided to enter this "brave new world" of eCommerce and participate in its success. But before you run off and open your online storefront, you should learn something of the basics of eCommerce.

To a newbie on the Internet, eCommerce appears to be a well-established fact. Commercials on radio and TV, ads on websites, and spam in their email box all contribute to this appearance. But in reality, buying online is a fairly recent phenomenon. It's been less than 10 years since the first eTailer opened its doors to the online consumer. Since then, it seems just about anyone with a product to sell or a service to offer has joined the land-rush to cyberspace, offering their wares to the almost one billion consumers on the Internet today.

Which raises the question, is there room for the newcomer? The answer is empathically yes!

But what about the dot-com crash a few years back, you ask? You may think that since the dot-com balloon became the dot-bomb bust, businesses are leery of eCommerce. But the truth is that many small businesses are conducting eCommerce quite successfully, thank you—they're small enough not to be noticed by CNN and MSNBC.

Why a Yahoo! Store?

The Internet is still an open marketplace for small startups, home businesses, and one-person operations that can *and* do build profitable online businesses. There's nothing really mysterious about eCommerce. If you ever bought an item from a catalog or from an advertisement in a magazine, the purchase process is pretty much the same. The only difference is that instead of purchasing from a person over the telephone or sending a check through the mail, you're conducting the transaction with a mouse through your PC and the Internet. For the business, the fulfillment process that takes place is no different from taking and fulfilling an order over the phone. For the buyer, the transaction is completed electronically and without human intervention. Note—just about all big catalog houses have moved their offerings to the Internet.

eCommerce offers advantages to both the buyer and seller.

Free Info   Download the free informative article titled "Dying Is Easy—eCommerce Is Hard" at www.MyEcommerceSuccess.com.

Advantages to the Online Buyer and Seller

The advantages to the online buyer include the ability to find hard-to-get items from the comfort of his or her chair, bargain pricing, and automated cost-comparison. In addition, the buyer can shop from the comfort of his or her home, 24 hours a day, 7 days a week, 365 days a year and never worry about finding a parking place. And with a click of the mouse, a buyer can search for the best prices on items using shopping comparison sites such as mySimon, Dealtime, and Froogle. The advantages for the seller include access to worldwide markets (the first W in World Wide Web is "world"), minimal sales costs, and the ability to track purchases and user data to recommend other items to the customer. Amazon is good example of "If you like this, you might want that."

Disadvantages to the Online Buyer and Seller

But all is not perfect in the online shopping world. The disadvantages to the buyer include no face-to-face exchanges with a merchant if questions arise, the hassle of shipping retuned goods to the merchant, and solving long-distance customer service problems. And for all its advantages to the online seller, an eCommerce business still faces the same challenges as those of physical businesses, such as building a digital presence, marketing and promoting the business, taking orders, fulfilling and shipping them, and tending to all the customer service issues that any business must solve.

Customer service, customer care, good products or services at a fair price, and above all, a good, well-thought-out business plan that is well executed are principles that still hold true in business whether online or not.

So, why is eCommerce so special? Why has it been such a success and growing in use every year with consumers?

eCommerce levels the playing field and lets small companies that have found a unique selling niche compete, literally, on a global scale. If you have the right kind of business, the Internet can open up a vast market of customers to you at an affordable price.

And that's the opportunity that Yahoo! stores offers.

Today's eShopper

Let's take a look at the average shopper as to age, gender, income, media habits, and dollar volume. The surveys of online shoppers have produced some very telling and interesting results.

People who shop online are older than you think and thus more affluent. eMarketer (www.emarketer.com) estimates that in 2005 there were 33.2 million people online in the U.S. between the ages of 50 and 64, triple the number of 65+ online users.

Income

The number of affluent Internet users in the U.S. is growing. Nielsen/NetRatings (www.netratings.com) estimated in 2005 that the number of Internet users in the U.S. with household income exceeding $150,000 would increase from about 8.6 million in 2004 to more than 10.3 million in 2005, a change of 19.8%.

Media Habits

BURST! Media (www.burstmedia.com) reported that in 2005 Internet users said they were spending more time online, and less with other media. More than 35% of respondents said they were watching less TV, and nearly as many said they were spending less time with magazines. Some 30.3% said newspapers were getting less of their attention. This shows that the consumer's media habits are changing, and changing fast. Companies see this migration from old media to new and are positioning themselves on the Internet to capture this new market attention. And so can you.

Web Resource

Staying Up to Date in eCommerce

There are many good sites on the Net that can keep you up to date on the happenings in eCommerce. Here are a few.

The eCommerce Times (www.ecommercetimes.com) and Internet Retailer (www.internetretailer.com) offer industry strategies for online merchants and provide daily news, articles, and research. ClickZ (www.clickz.com) offers expert advice on Internet, email, brand, and interactive marketing. Subscribe to these organization's newsletters and receive an eCommerce seminar in your email box everyday.

We have a website that offers Yahoo! store updates, marketing and promotion ideas and service for your Yahoo! store, instructional videos on how to set up and manage a Yahoo! store, and a Yahoo! store customization service that will create a unique look and feel for your Yahoo! store with additional storefront elements not provided with a standard Yahoo! store. Find our site at MyEcommerceSuccess.com.

Revenue and Sales

Sales are increasing too.

In 2004, Forrester Research (www.forrester.com) estimated that total retail online spending in general merchandise will reach $151.3 billion by 2010, up from $75.7 billion this year. Those numbers exclude online ticket sales projected by Forrester at $9.4 billion in 2010, up from $4.3 billion this year. Forrester projects additional online sales of about $155.5 billion in 2010 from the combined category of automobiles and auto parts/food and beverages/travel, up from $65.6 billion for the category this year. Forrester also projected that new households going online and more online spending from those already there will drive up consumer spending on the Internet to account for about 13% of all general merchandise retail spending by 2010.

The gender demographics are shifting as well. More women have come to the Internet and are making an impact on eCommerce. According to Media

Metrix, in 2001, women made up slightly more than half of the online population in America. More than a third of online women are between the ages of 18 and 55.

All of these statistics prove that there is a vast market online to be tapped by anyone who has a good product or service to sell at a fair price.

Yahoo! Stores—Empowering eCommerce

A Yahoo! store can give your business the look and feel of a large business. But it does something more important. Can you set up and run an online storefront by slapping together the parts of an eCommerce website from different organizations and companies on the Web? Sure. You can set up a free website from the several free website companies on the Web, add a shopping cart from some eCommerce solution company, do some free advertising on discussion lists, post some notices on discussion groups, and buy an email list to promote your business with.

You will soon find that this patchwork approach will not only cause problems and inconsistent service, but does not project a professional look for your business. The Yahoo! Stores program provides a comprehensive, integrated, one-stop shop for creating a credible online business (see Figure 1.1).

FIGURE 1.1

College Sports Stuff is only one of the many small online businesses satisfied with the Yahoo! Store solution. "The templates were easy and if I had any problems, I knew I could call the support group—they gave us the answer immediately."

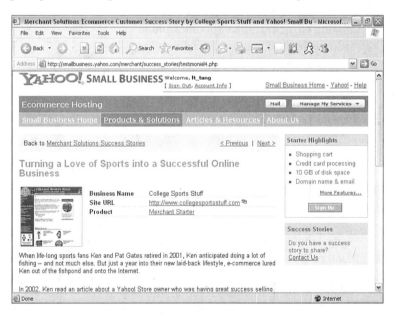

o how do you make a buck online? Well, there are several sources that an online store can use to generate revenue using several revenue models. In addition to revenue from selling products or services, revenue sources could also include selling advertising such as banner ads or sponsorships on your website or selling subscriptions to information such as newsletters or electronic magazines. But if eCommerce was easy, as easy as that, everyone would be doing it. To be successful at eCommerce a business must be able to perform quite a few tasks.

The first one is the most important: Even before you even think of creating your online storefront, you need to develop a reason why consumers should come to your website. If you're successful at creating such a draw, you must have a digital presence that encourages shoppers to browse your offerings. Once you've done that, you have to convince the shopper to complete a transaction by offering easy-to-find products or services.

Other considerations include a secure and reliable company to host your online storefront; an easy to set up and maintain eCommerce website; an online shopping cart; a way to take and process credit cards online; the ability to ship products or download information; a "back office" to track your business and monitor how much money your website has made where you can make real-time website design changes, monitor your database, and more; and, of course, a well thought-out marketing strategy.

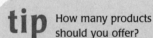 **tip** How many products should you offer?

You don't need to have hundreds of products to sell to have a successful eCommerce business. Many successful online businesses sell fewer than 20 products. Yahoo! Store has found that adding more items to a store does not guarantee more sales. Yahoo! Stores that sold fewer than 10 products had almost as many sales as those stores selling 50 or more.

The remaining parts of this book will show you, by using the Yahoo! store technology, how easily and cost effectively you can perform the tasks necessary to create, maintain, and promote a world-class eCommerce website.

But a Yahoo! store can only provide the tools for success. In order to actually become a success in eCommerce, you need to be aware of the three Cs of eCommerce.

The Three Cs of eCommerce

A successful online storefront does more than just sell product or services. It offers fresh content applicable to products and services it sells and a way to interact with shoppers and customers. These important elements of an online storefront are known as the three Cs of eCommerce and must be considered to make your online store more of a success.

- **Content**—When merchants think of content on the online store, they think primarily of product or service descriptions. But separate content that is relevant to your target audience is also an important part of an eCommerce site.

- **Community**—Site visitor interaction with each other and your company through discussion boards and other forums of discussion makes shoppers feel part of your business.

- **Commerce**—What you sell but also the other ways to monetize, or make money from, shoppers who visit your site.

That's the eCommerce site equation: Content builds community interaction—something to talk about—which establishes credibility with shoppers, which generates sales from visitors to your online store. The proper integration of content, community and commerce will entice shoppers to come back to your storefront and buy more from you again and again. If you're successful applying the 3 Cs, you will develop a following of shoppers and customers that will turn into sales.

Let's take a look at the 3 Cs.

Content: Providing Fish Food

People use the Net to learn and good content will attract them to your storefront. If it's interesting enough and if you took care to provide content that is refreshed periodically, it will make visitors come to your site, stay, and keep coming back for more.

But content serves another purpose, a very important one. Search engines love content. The more content you have on your online store, the better chance search engines will find your site. And if you optimize your site content pages properly (see Chapter 12, "Search Engine Optimization and Listing"), your site will show up high in search engine results.

Does your site content have to be directly related to your product or service? Not necessarily. The purpose of content is to provide information that meets your shoppers' needs and desires. A good online store is not only a place to buy, but a place to learn, too. While learning, visitors linger and soon become buyers. For example, take a pool chemical supply company that sells online. Its content could educate consumers in the proper use of pool chemicals, how to use them and in what quantity, and so forth. But the business could also have content on its site that speaks about pool safety for children. A person looking for animation on pool safety might find his or her way to the pool site and then become a customer.

There are four types of content that you can place on your eCommerce site to become

- The Referrer
- The Informer
- The Advisor
- The Context Provider

The Referrer: You're the expert when it comes to knowing the products or services you sell. So use this knowledge to help your visitors understand all aspects of your product or service. Take the time to research the information your site visitors might want to know, and then create an "Additional Resources" section in your online store that points to places on the Web that your visitors and shoppers will find useful.

For example, suppose you sell computer products. In your additional resources section, list content sites, community sites, and discussion boards where shoppers can find reviews comparing one product you may sell to another. That would be a very time-consuming task. Instead, you could refer your customers to sites that specialize in these reviews, such as ZDNet, CNET, and TechTV (see Figure 1.2). Or suppose you sell furniture or other home décor. You can refer visitors to your online store to companies that provide design ideas and project estimators.

The Informer: Make your site a place for news and opinions on your market and product or service niche. Articles, opinions, even a reminder service can inform shoppers to your online store of what's new in your marketplace.

Providing what's new in your market niche on a regular basis will entice shoppers to return to your store time and time again.

FIGURE 1.2

CNET is known for its expert reviews on everything technology. Whether it's personal electronics, computer gear, digital cameras, or hosting and Internet service providers, they review them and tell you the best in class.

http://www.cnet.com

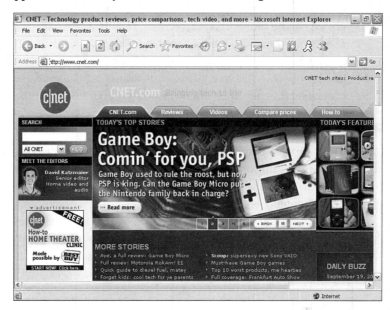

YellowBrix provides a wealth of free content from hundreds of content sources including news, weather, sports, business, entertainment, and technology news (see Figure 1.3).

FIGURE 1.3

YellowBrix is a leading provider of real-time syndicated news services and web content solutions. Use them to find content that you can place on your online store.

http://www.yellowbrix.com/

The Advisor: Many shoppers need advice to make a buying decision. By acting as a trusted advisor, you not only build confidence with shoppers, but also increase the possibility of making a sale. A good example of this kind of advice can be found at Amazon.com. They pioneered the concept of reader reviews for the books they sell and video reviews for their videos. Anyone who has purchased the product can write his or her own review. A peer review looks more objective to a potential customer and increases the possibility of a purchase; shoppers trust other consumers' opinions more than they trust advertisers. Ask visitors to your site to email you their peer reviews of your product or service.

The Context Provider: Another way to provide content on your storefront is by offering informational tools to help shoppers make buying decisions. Consider giving shoppers the capability of solving a problem or determining their shopping needs in the context of your site using online tools such as checklists, calculators, evaluators, and simulators. Context-specific information can be either product-specific (helping potential customers make a buying decision at your site) or shopping-specific (such as links to currency exchanges, international holiday listings, and a world time calculator).

Community: Staying Connected

People go online not just to be informed but also to interact with other people. Filling this need at your web store will help you turn shoppers into customers and customers into repeat buyers. Content can attract shoppers to your site. But to generate a continuous flow of repeat visitors, you need to provide access to an interactive community of some type.

tip Another benefit of a newsletter is that it can add valuable content to your site by posting it and archiving older newsletters. Again, search engines love content and this will aid them finding your online storefront.

An electronic newsletter sent out periodically to customers and prospects can keep your subscribers informed about what's new on your site. You can announce new features, new products, or new promotions that can be used to drive subscribers back to your site on a regular basis. Use your newsletter to nurture potential customers until they're ready to purchase a product from you or sign a contract.

Asking questions, discussing problems, raising issues, and the general camaraderie that develops in an interactive community breeds a kind of loyalty that's beneficial to the success of your web store. And loyalty breeds repeat visits.

Another way to engage your customers and prospects interactively is through the use of discussion lists. A discussion list is a discussion board via email. Subscribers to your discussion list receive email on a regular basis containing comments that are echoed to every subscriber on the list. A well-executed discussion list can gain wide visibility and a very good reputation for your business and for the products or services you sell. The easiest and free way to add a discussion list to your eCommerce strategy is by using Yahoo! Groups. You can create a discussion list by using their free Yahoo! Groups service. You can even use Yahoo! Groups to compile and send out your periodic newsletter.

Yahoo Talk   **What are Yahoo! Groups?**

Yahoo! Groups (groups.yahoo.com) is a FREE electronic mailing list service provided by Yahoo!. It's one the easiest ways for companies to communicate with prospects and customers on the Internet.

Commerce: More Than One Way to Skin a Dollar

There's more than one way to make money with your online store. This is done by creating multiple revenue streams. Adding different revenue streams to your site will leverage your site traffic and generate additional income. For example

- **What you primarily sell**—This is the main revenue stream of your web store. It's what you built your e-business around and should be your prime focus.

- **Sell advertising**—If you've built up a considerable level of visitors to your site on a regular basis, you can consider turning some of that traffic into revenue. Advertisers are always looking for ways to get their product or service message out to potential customers. They know that placing ads on websites that cater to shoppers who might buy their product is a wise way to spend their advertising dollars.

- **Become a Referrer**—You generate additional revenue by referring your shoppers to a non-competitive merchant in exchange for a percentage of the sale.

Develop several of these income streams simultaneously, and you can grow your site revenue beyond your product or service offers.

Now that you've passed eCommerce 101, so to speak, it's time to identify a customer need to target your eCommerce business. If you already have a business, it still would be worthwhile to read the next chapter to refine your target customer and sharpen your strategy on how to sell to them.

Choosing a Product or Service

Most people who open a Yahoo! store know in advance what they're going sell. Some choose a product that they know, have, or can source, or a service that they can provide. Others may not have a specific product or service in mind but want to join in and benefit from the eCommerce revolution.

Every business, no matter what it sells, must find a way to create a unique selling position to compete in the world of eCommerce. That unique selling position, or USP, consists of two parts—a *customer niche* and a *market niche*. We'll discuss the market niche and unique selling positions in more detail in the next chapter. In this chapter we'll focus on the first step of creating that effective USP for your online business.

Even if you already have an ongoing home business that you wish to bring online, you will find the process described here and in the next chapter valuable to the success of your online business and ascertaining whether you are targeting your product or service properly. For without a well-defined, effective USP built directly into the design of your online storefront and the creation of content that reflects it, you will find it exceedingly difficult to effectively promote and market your finished online storefront as we move through the steps of launching your Yahoo! store.

> **tip** **Do What You Enjoy**
>
> People start a business to make money. After all, that's a business's purpose. But it's important for you to pick a business that you enjoy. You may make a lot of money running a business you don't love, but the mental anguish of working at a business you don't enjoy is a high price to pay. Many entrepreneurs running successful businesses are unhappy doing it. The end result is that some literally make themselves sick.

Selling to Human Motivations

Most business people make the mistake of thinking they should look for a *product* to sell when they should be looking for a *market* to sell to. Here are some basic criteria to keep in mind when choosing a customer niche.

First of all, products don't buy from you—people do. That means first focus on a target market of people and what human needs you are going to fill. Another way to look at it is finding a pain in the marketplace and curing it. What negative aspect of the marketplace in terms of a product or service can you identify? Then offer a solution.

Free Info   Download the free informative article titled "The Secret to eCommerce Success—Imitate, Don't Innovate" at www.MyEcommerceSuccess.com.

Second, make sure it's your target customer's passion, not yours. The target market you choose, the human need you will fill, must be passionate about the problem you are going to solve or the need you are going to fill and back that passion up with good money to pay for your solution. There are all kinds of people who are passionate about a variety of subjects but are unwilling to spend money on them. In other words, money talks, baloney walks.

Another way to look at customer passion is shopper motivation. That is, what motivates a shopper to buy? Different shoppers are motivated by different things, even at different times. When trying to choose a product or service to sell, keep the following human motivators in mind:

- Need for information
- Economic motivations
- Need to be entertained
- Social motivations

If the Internet is known for anything, it's information. That's where the Internet shines. And the need for information is a great human motivator. The Internet is like the Library of Congress multiplied millions of times. But it's also a vast information storehouse that is hard to navigate. Provide a ready source of information that meets a shopper's needs, and you can turn that shopper into a customer.

Economics is a strong motivator. It goes without saying that commerce on the Net is a fast growing segment. After all, if you didn't believe that, you wouldn't be reading this book! And what is the economic motivator? A quality product at a fair price, a nice selection, and a secure and convenient way to buy. All these and more would entice a shopper to open his wallet and buy from your online store.

Entertainment is another motivator. We all love to be entertained. We'll even pay for it if we feel the value is there. So think about ways of selling entertainment products and services to the online shopper.

> **tip** **Go to the Horse's Mouth**
>
> Check out the many discussion boards, message boards, and blogs on the Web and ask your target market what they need or what problems they would like to be solved. Yahoo! Groups at groups.yahoo.com is a great place to start. Type your target market into the search window on the Yahoo! Groups home page and see what groups show up. Then visit their message boards and read what they say. Take the keyword "Kid Toys," for example. Type that into the search window and you'll see dozens of different discussion groups that focus on kid's toys. Ask the group what "needs" they see in their toy category. What do people buy and why? What do they want to buy but can't? What do they buy and don't like? What are they buying a lot of? What's trendy and in vogue?

Finally, human interaction is a strong motivational force. The opportunity to hobnob with those of similar interests can be turned into a profitable business. Think about community sites that provide live chat or ways for people to meet one another. Fill the need to interact and you can build an effective business on it.

Selling to Human Needs

Many years ago, a psychologist by the name of Abraham Maslow spent a lot of time categorizing human needs. Dr. Maslow organized our human needs into four categories:

- Physical needs
- Safety needs
- Belonging needs
- Esteem needs

If he were alive today and on the Internet, I bet he would have created a pretty successful Yahoo! store. Using his list of human needs, he would be very good at choosing products or services to satisfy them.

Let's see how well we can do.

Selling to Physical Needs

The basic physical human needs are food, shelter, and clothing. If you were going to sell products or services that satisfy these physical needs, you could consider these types of products and services.

Let's look first at some *products* that can satisfy our physical needs.

We all need to eat and drink, so selling food products online is a natural. It's something that we all need, and better yet, it's consumable. That means it's a product that people buy over and over again. That's good for a business. If you're selling food, your product can be gourmet in nature, or ethnic or regional food types that certain customer segments would want to buy (see Figure 2.1).

The need for shelter from the elements is right up there with sustenance. Outdoor products such as camping and hunting gear and goods for the patio and garden make very good merchandise to sell at a Yahoo! store (see Figure 2.2).

Finally, though we might not buy clothing as often as we do food, covering our bodies is a social necessity. Apparel both meets the needs of the fashion conscious and protects us from the elements.

What about services? Which ones can satisfy our physical needs? Many who eat also cook. Providing consumer information on how to cook, what to cook, and where to cook is a very good service to sell online, such as an "Ask Mr. Chef" site where consumers can ask cooking questions of expert chefs.

FIGURE 2.1

This Northwest Gourmet corporate gift basket features the best gourmet foods of the Northwest.

FIGURE 2.2

Tents, Etc. sells primarily tents, at a discount.

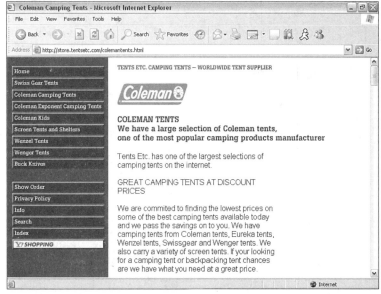

Here's another idea. We all eat out. Many of us eat out frequently. An online business that lists and categorizes restaurants and their reviews is another service that can be provided online and can meet human physical needs.

Take clothing and shelter. A Yahoo! store could provide a directory of the best places to camp in an area or a list of places to fish and hunt. One might even include the ways to catch, clean, and cook the fish and game that you get.

You then have a site that does double duty: where to hunt and fish and how to cook what you catch. Sell this kind of information and you have a business.

FIGURE 2.3

Restaurant Ratingz provides reviews and ratings of restaurants and cafés in your community. You can even write your own reviews.

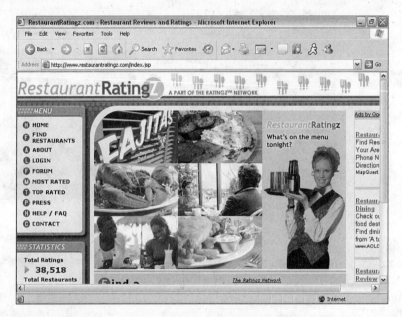

Selling to Safety Needs

Feeling safe and secure is one of our strongest basic needs. The safety needs of protecting self, family, and home offer an online business the opportunity to sell a variety of merchandise and a nice selection of services to the online consumer. An additional safety concern is our health. Think about these product and service ideas if this is the type of human need that you wish to satisfy.

Let's start with product ideas that satisfy safety needs.

Security products such as self-defense items and security devices to use when traveling would make very good products to sell at a Yahoo! store (see Figure 2.4). Books and tapes on self-defense are other product ideas. Child safety products such as baby seats and identification systems would sell well, along with home safes and surveillance equipment.

Diet books, exercise tapes, and health and nutrition products are very big sellers on the Net. First-aid equipment and home medical supplies also are good products to sell as well as products for people with disabilities.

What about services?

Many types of safety services can be delivered online and would make a low-overhead, profitable business. They would include private investigative services, directories of alarm services and their reviews, and emergency alert services for the infirm and elderly (see Figure 2.5). Another service idea would be to provide nutrition and health information. Weight-loss information; nutrition services and guides; and even life, auto, and health insurance can be profitable services sold at a Yahoo! store.

FIGURE 2.4

Safe-Mart sells a security system for the home.

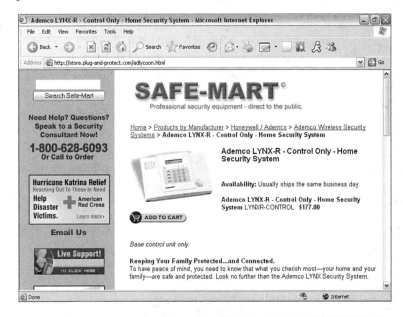

FIGURE 2.5

911 Broadcast offers emergency alert phone systems and services for contacting members of a community or organization in the event of an emergency.

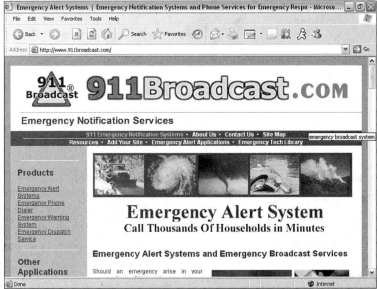

Selling to Belonging Needs

To be loved, to have friends, and to be part of a family fulfill our need to be a part of something greater than ourselves. This need to belong and to express our appreciation for being part of something important offers a variety of online business opportunities.

Gift giving can satisfy the need to belong and express our affection for lovers, friends, and family. Online gift shops are a natural for the Net (see Figure 2.6). When people want to express their affections in a more tangible manner, gifts are one of the best ways to do it. Other products that do just as well are the traditional flowers, cards, and candy. Any of these should be considered as merchandise ideas for your online business.

FIGURE 2.6

Grandma's Gift Baskets sell gifts baskets for all occasions.

Service ideas could include establishing a gift registry service. This type of service enables visitors to your storefront to list the actual gifts they want and then inform the potential gift givers. You can either sell the gifts directly or send orders to a gift house that would fulfill and ship them to your customers. Another good example of servicing belonging needs is a genealogy service. Tracing one's roots has become very popular over the last several years. And of course, another popular service that meets the belonging need is an online dating service.

Selling to Esteem Needs

We all like to gain recognition and feel good about ourselves. Products and services that cater to our esteem needs offer a great opportunity for an online business. How we feel about ourselves and how others perceive us is important to us. Recognition and vanity are strong personal needs that we seek to fulfill.

Beauty and grooming items and other personal care merchandise are the most popular products to sell if your online business is targeting the esteem needs of the consumer. For women, perfume, bath and body lotions, cosmetics, and even fashion products are key items to sell (see Figure 2.7). For men, cologne, razors, and electric shavers would fill the bill.

FIGURE 2.7

StrawberryNet sells women's cosmetics for any occasion.

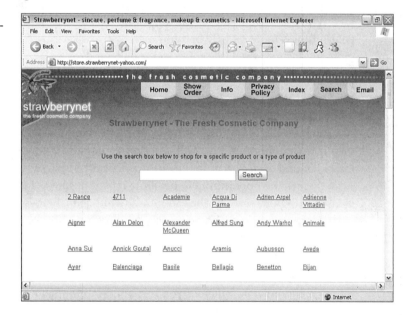

Other products that "stroke" our esteem are jewelry items for the ladies such as rings, diamonds, bracelets, and precious stones, and for men, watches, cufflinks, and rings. Then there are books and videos on personal care, dieting, and products to reverse the aging process.

Services that satisfy esteem needs include training and educational courses. Many of these can be easily offered online, such as computer certification classes or real estate courses. You can sell beauty tips to your customers or offer a jewelry appraisal service. Finally, you can offer advice on how to succeed in business or even, after reading this book, offer a course on how to set up your own Yahoo! store!

Should I Sell a Product or Service?

That's a good question. Luckily you can do either one with a Yahoo! store. It makes no difference whether you sell a product or a service from your Yahoo! store. Both have their advantages and disadvantages.

Selling products online has certain advantages. When selling products, you're not constrained by a limited amount of inventory. When selling products, you can grow your business more quickly because the more products you sell, the more income you make.

The disadvantage of selling products is that they normally require you to stock and ship them.

Ana Ricon, the About Guide to Online Business at onlinebusiness.about.com, speaks about the importance of supply and demand for the products you plan to sell. The advantage of an online services company is that making a profit is quicker and easier because the entire price of the service is paid to you. Also, there is the opportunity to generate repeat business if your clients are pleased with your service. The main disadvantage is there is only so much *time*. We're only human and a person can perform only a certain number of services in a 24-hour period.

Selling services can provide you with immediate revenue but will never give you the biggest bang for your buck in the long run. In short, you can sell only so much of your time, whereas you can sell an unlimited amount of products. The trick is to turn a successful online service into a product. An example is to have a service that helps people market their online business, such as Internet marketing, and then sell them a book on how to do it themselves.

Zero In on Your Product or Service

As in any business, supply and demand determine what products or services succeed in the marketplace and which ones do not. Internet search engines can give you an approximation of how frequently people search for your product. There are a number of online tools that when used together can help you decide whether the product or service you have in mind is really in demand by consumers and what the supply for it is—that is, how many businesses are selling the product or service.

Here's what to do.

1. Go to Google's Keyword Sandbox at https://adwords.google.com/select/ KeywordSandbox. The Google Keyword Sandbox is a great little keyword suggestion tool that you can use to see the popularity of your product or service. For example, suppose you want to sell baby toys. Type the phrase "baby toys" into the search box on the Keyword Sandbox page. Google will return a large list of suggested terms. Choose a few that are relevant and targeted to your product or business. Sometimes, to the right, you'll see related terms and common misspellings. Note these, too.

2. Go to the Overture Term Suggestion Tool at http://inventory.overture.com/d/searchinventory/suggestion/. Take the keyword terms that you found at the Google Keyword Sandbox, enter one of the terms in the search term suggestion tool, and see how many people have searched for that term, and any combination of the terms or keyword, over the last 30 days. Overture will help slice and dice the keywords for your product or service and help you better describe the product or service you wish to offer.

3. Go to the Google search engine at http://www.google.com, enter one of your popular search terms or keywords identified by the Overture tool, and see how many websites appear under that search term. Your objective is to target keywords most frequently used by your target audience but with the least amount of competing pages. *Important*: Be specific with your search terms and keywords. For example, using the keyword phrase "baby toys" produces a number of different search terms at the Overture tool, such as "educational baby toy" and "baby learning toy." Using these terms at Google will help you see competitive variations on your product.

4. Finally, find out who your competitors are. Go to Yahoo! Stores at shopping.yahoo.com, enter your product or service, and you will see how many companies you may be competing with in your product or service area.

Web Resource

Streamlining Your Research

A product that streamlines this research is The Market Research Wizard (e-comprofits.com/ marketresearch.html). This program analyzes the factors mentioned above, and then rates the probability of successful sales on the Internet. It is very useful for comparing the relative ranking of different products. I like the product, but it takes time to arrive at the best combination of keywords. The free trial is limited to five searches. The registered program costs $97.

This four-part process can help you see what products and services are in demand and who, if anyone, is offering them.

Choosing an Online Business

Though choosing an online business may seem complex at first, there are basically three ways to sell through an online storefront.

> **tip** **Can't Think of a Product to Sell? Try This**
>
> You've tried and tried, but still can't come up with a product to sell. Why not find a merchant who already is selling products, but *not* online, and offer to sell them on the Net? You create the site, the merchant supplies the product, and you both make money

- Start from scratch. You don't have to limit yourself to selling other people's products or even services. Consider selling your own creative work. Or maybe a service. Ask yourself this: What one thing do you do better than everyone else? Maybe you're a good photographer. Or perhaps you enjoy writing. Maybe you enjoy working with your hands, creating works of art or unique items that can be sold as gifts. You can also create your own information products such as ebooks or music files and sell them to consumers.

  Sit down some evening with a pad and pencil or drop by your local coffeehouse and make a list of what you enjoy doing. You might be surprised that what you like to do can be turned into a product or service you can sell online. The key thought here again is to do what you enjoy!

- The second way to start an online business is through the traditional retail model. Buy products from wholesale distributors and resell them for a profit. If you'd rather not stock inventory at your home business then have the distributors drop ship your products from their warehouse. You take the orders; they do the shipping. You can also buy your products from local businesses. You may find businesses in your neighborhood that sell products, but do not have an eCommerce storefront. Approach them and offer to sell their product online in exchange for a percentage of the profits. A good example of this is the local crafters. They are a good source of unique products, and may be willing to sell to you at wholesale if you purchase in quantity. You can either buy the item outright or set up a consignment arrangement with them.

■ Finally, there's no reason why you couldn't combine two or three of these online business approaches into one online storefront.

Once you've targeted your customer niche and the type of products or services you want to offer, it's time to decide upon a market niche and that most important part of your unique selling position. Turn the page and let's move on.

CHAPTER

3

Creating a Unique Selling Position

Once you've chosen your target customer and the needs you plan to fill, the next step is to create a unique selling position, or USP, for your product or service. In order to zero in on an effective and useful USP, we need to look at three types of market criteria. They are

- WIIFM (What's In It For Me)

- The Four Ps

- The Big Five

We'll talk at the end of this chapter on how the integration of the customer niche and market niche criteria, if done properly, will give your USP more than just the sum of its parts. For the USP must be designed into the online storefront, not after it's up and running.

What's In It for Me?

The last thingyou want visitors to say to themselves when they view your carefully constructed offer at your online storefront is "So what? What's in it to me?" It could be that you're not answering the ever-present question of the online shopper, "What's in it for me?" And you have to answer it in less than 10 seconds or they're off to your competitor.

Many years ago, a company called Federal Express (www.fedex.com) came up with a new concept: delivering packages overnight. Until FedEx came along, if you wanted to ship a small package to the next city or state or even across the country, you had to go down to either the local bus station, post office, or airport and hand the small package over to the bus company, post office, or airline for them to deliver it. You were pretty much at the mercy of these shipping companies who would deliver the package on their schedule, not yours. Back then it might take up to several days to have your package delivered because the bus companies and airlines were in the business of moving people or, in the case of the airlines, people and large cargo, not small packages. Then, it had to be picked up at the package's final destination! And though the post office would deliver small parcels, you never really knew when they would be delivered.

FedEx saw an opportunity here. All they had to do was convince the public that they could deliver packages in a convenient and speedier fashion. But they needed a slogan that would say that their package delivery service was better than those of the airlines and bus companies. And they needed to say it in one simple phrase.

Free Info   Download the free informative article titled "The Seven Cardinal Virtues of eCommerce" at www.MyEcommerceSuccess.com.

After much thought, they decided that what differentiated them from their competitors was that they owned their own planes. This meant that customers could ship and receive products on the customer's schedule, and not the schedule of the airlines or buses. So what was the unique selling position that FedEx chose? *We have our own planes.*

It didn't fly with the public.

People didn't get it. "So you have your own planes," they said. "What does that mean to me?"

So, FedEx went back to the drawing board and came up with this: "When you absolutely, positively have to have it overnight." That worked. The public responded, and the rest is commerce history. Consumers didn't care if FedEx had their own planes. They didn't care if their packages were delivered by plane, train, bus, car, or Pony Express. The benefit to the consumer was that the package was delivered overnight, right to the recipient's door.

Another good example is Domino's Pizza (www.dominos.com). How do you differentiate one pizza service from another? Domino's differentiated itself when it first got started from the competition by promising to deliver your pizza in record time: "30 minutes or less, or it's free!"

There's a lesson here, one that you can use when creating your own unique selling position (USP). You need to always remember WIIFM: "What's in it for me?" This is what a customer is looking for when he or she buys. Phrase your USP in those terms and you'll go a long way in creating an effective and successful unique selling position.

Differentiating Yourself from Your Competition

It's a competitive world out there, and getting more so every day. Your business is faced with the challenge of differentiating itself from your competitors and giving the consumer a reason why they should buy from you rather than your competition. But that's not as easy as it seems.

For example, ask a random sample of business owners to tell you what makes them different from their competition, and you'll get a blank stare, or perhaps a response like one of these:

"My prices are the lowest."

"I guarantee satisfaction."

"My products are of high quality."

"I give great customer service."

But none of these responses sets them apart from the competition. Many businesses can claim the same things. A business must know what they offer a customer besides general statements and why they think a shopper should buy from them. That is, what makes the business unique in the market and in the eyes of a potential customer? To do that, you need to ask yourself the following questions.

- What gives your company a unique *advantage* over your competition?
- What is the distinct *reason* for consumers to buy from you?
- Can you portray in the consumer's mind a compelling *image* of what your business will do for them that others can't?

Notice those highlighted words: advantage, reason, and image. That's your objective when creating a solid, exact, and usable unique selling position that both positions you in the marketplace and convinces a consumer to buy from you. A good USP creates the framework and lays the foundation for your compelling product or service offer.

If that isn't enough, a good USP also keeps your business pointed in the right direction.

One of the things that made both FedEx and Domino's a success was a *measurable* and *beneficial* USP. They were measurable (overnight and 30 minutes, respectively) and carried a unique benefit (FedEx delivers to the recipient's door; Domino's promises it's free if not delivered on time).

Getting the picture? A good USP is specific, measurable, and conveys a customer benefit. Let's review.

So how do you differentiate yourself from the competition? How do you answer the consumer questions of WIIFM? Start with this: Using a pad and pencil, ask yourself the following questions and answer them as simply as you can. Remember, you're not creating a corporate mission statement here, so keep your responses simple.

"Why is my business special?"

"Why would someone buy from me instead of my competition?"

"What can my business provide to a consumer that no one else can?"

"What's a benefit to the consumer that I can deliver on?"

Keep your answers simple, specific, and measurable, and show a benefit to the buyer. If you're confused by what you offer, your customers will be, too.

Keeping Your Eye on the Competition

Ignorance may be bliss, but in the knock-down, drag-out world of business, ignorance of your competition can be a deadly mistake.

Keeping track of your competitors can be a difficult and time-consuming task. You can hire a corporate spy to infiltrate your competitor's organization; do a little dumpster-diving for useful discarded memos, manuals, and correspondence; or work smart by monitoring your competition's activities right from your desk, using the Internet. The Internet is filled with resources that can provide your company with media sources, web directories, clipping services, and competitive intelligence to keep you up to date on who the competition is and what they're doing.

By using these online sources, you can discover the answers to questions such as

"Who are the leading companies in your industry?"

"What information on your competition is available?"

"Which of your competitors are most likely threats?"

Positioning Your Business— The Marketing Mix

> **tip** **Mix & Match**
>
> Think of the criteria of the Four Ps as variables that you can control. The Four Ps are interdependent upon each other, and taken together they form a marketing mix. Your objective is to come up with a mix of these Ps that will clearly differentiate you from the competition.

If you've been anywhere near a marketing course, you would have heard of the Four Ps of Marketing. They are price, place, product and promotion. The Four Ps is another set of criteria that can help you choose a market niche. Let's look at price first.

If you're going to compete on *price*, don't just say you're the lowest—say why. Customers will not accept a blanket statement unless you can prove it. For instance, perhaps you can sell at such a low price because of your ability to source product from the closeout industry, buying products at pennies on the dollar. Or perhaps you have an exclusive arrangement with a distributor or manufacturer that no one else has, allowing you to sell at the lowest price. On the other hand, you may sell at the highest price but offer some added value, such as free shipping or free 24/7 support. Play up these unique factors in your USP.

Next is *place*. The Marines are a good example of this P.

The Marines are looking for a few good men—not all men, just a few, and only good ones. This is a great positioning statement, which makes their "business" unique and differentiates them among the other services of the armed forces. Another example was the tagline "The Pepsi Generation."

Look for a similar positioning with your business. Perhaps your focus is gender-based. Perhaps it's age-based. Sell to a unique segment of the population, not to all of it.

Following place is *product*. Take a common product that others sell and repackage it in a new way. For instance, take the iMac. It's just a PC, but look at the packaging. Not only does it sell, but it sells at a premium price! It also has a great positioning statement. *Think Different!* The iPod is another example. There are portable music devices at a lesser price, but Apple has learned that a sexy package goes a long way in differentiating the product, plus carrying a higher price tag.

Then there's *promotion*. Study the promotional possibilities of your product or service. Can you tie your product or service with a season or holiday where you can benefit from the promotional activities and mindshare of consumers that already exist at that time of year? Targeting your promotional message at the right time is the key to acceptance. So sit down and make a list of the popular seasonal events, including religious and cultural events other than those with a Euro-Christian focus, such as the Jewish and Asian religious holidays and ethnic holidays like Kwanzaa.

Finally, remember this very important fact when constructing your USP. Your USP is not about you nor is it about your business—it's about your customer.

caution
Promises, Promises.

Whatever you promise in your unique selling position, be sure you can deliver on it. Don't make the mistake of adopting a USP that you can't fulfill. This means making sure that everyone in your entire organization knows and understands your USP and can act on it!

The Big Five of eCommerce

Shoppers don't care about your site, your business, or your life. What they care about is themselves. When they come to your site, they want to see if there's anything there that interests them. They want to know, "What's in it for me!" They come to your web store with a certain set of expectations. Your job as a web merchant is to meet those expectations.

caution
It's the Customer, Stupid

Everything on your site should be about the customer and designed from the customer's point of view. Your customer not only needs a reason to buy, but to buy easily and safely.

Your customers expect to find what they came for: a fair price, a good selection of product, great service, and a secure and safe place to shop. In other words, they're looking for the Big Five of online shopping. And if they're from "out of town"—that is, another country—they're also looking for a site that speaks their language!

The Big Five are

- Selection
- Price
- Service

- Convenience
- Security

Consumers want to know right away if their visit to your site is going to save them time and money and if their shopping experience will be a pleasant one. Can they find what they want easily? Can they place an order in a variety of ways? Can they find your customer service pages, shipping and handling fees, and return policies without spending a large amount of time digging through your site looking for them?

These are the customer's expectations and you have to meet them if you want your online business to be a success. If your site is designed with the Big Five of online shopping in mind, you'll provide your customers a pleasant shopping experience and a reason to buy from your online store again.

Let's take a look at them. The Big Five of online shopping are selection, price, service, convenience, and security.

Selection: Do You Have What They Want?

Shoppers come to the Net for the vast selection of product and services that are available at the click of a mouse. Whether shoppers find you through search engines, store directories, or through your own marketing and promotion, after they arrive at your site, they want to know you have what they're looking for. Don't build an impression in the shoppers' mind that you sell computer software or have an online bookstore and then offer only a small selection of titles.

When building a small- to medium-sized business, you need to focus your product or service offering. Look at your unique selling position. If done correctly, it tells you the market you're targeting and the unique product or service you're selling. If you've done your homework and created a compelling unique selling position, the shopper will feel that your web store offers the best selection on the Net.

Store Examples

Offering a good selection to shoppers is not necessarily a numbers game. The quality of your selection is much more important for a small web business than the quantity. The following are some good examples of small sites that work in large product categories yet deliver a good selection of product offerings for their market.

Music Stores   You don't have to be a CDNow.com or an Amazon.com to be successful selling music CDs on the Web. Acres of Videos & CDs at Click4Stuff at stores.yahoo.com/ggroup sells hard-to-find CD sets. Shoppers who come to their web store will find a good product selection specializing in hard-to-find classic music CD sets. Aramusic at stores.yahoo.com/ara-music sells Arabic music CDs from the Middle East (see Figure 3.1). And Harmony Marketplace at stores.yahoo.com/harmonymarketplace carries the best in harmony music on CDs.

FIGURE 3.1
Aramusic has picked a narrow niche of the market. Middle Eastern music.

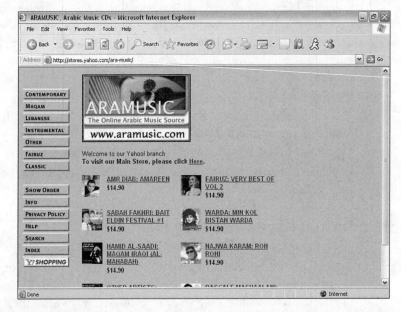

Software Stores   You don't have to be a CompUSA (www.compusa.com) to competitively sell software on the Net. You can offer a specialized selection of software to shoppers and still give them a good selection in the category you choose. AccountingShop at stores.yahoo.com/2020software sells only accounting software, whereas Natara Software at shop.store.yahoo.com/natara/ sells productivity software for the Palm handheld platform (see Figure 3.2).

Pet Stores   The large pet stores on the Net such as PetsMart (www.petsmart.com) carry a wide variety of pet supplies for all kinds of pets. But a small store such as BunnyLuv-Essentials at shop.store.yahoo.com/shopbunnyluv/ offers a nice selection of rabbit care supplies, toys, hay, food, and grooming tools. A shopper who comes to their site would be pleased with the selection of products in that subject area. Houndz in the Hood at stores.yahoo.com/houndzinthehood (see Figure 3.3) offers only coats for dachshunds, mini poodles, and Italian greyhounds. As you can see, you can run with the big dogs of eCommerce if you choose your product or service well and deliver the best selection in that category.

FIGURE 3.2

Natara Software chose to specialize on software made only for Palm PDAs.

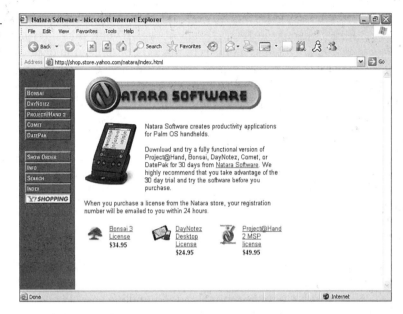

FIGURE 3.3

Houndz in the Hood saw a niche unfilled by a large section of dog coats and filled it.

Price: Is Your Price Right?

What kind of price animal is your eBusiness? That's a question you need to answer. And after you answer it, your web store must demonstrate it.

Do you sell products or services at a discount? Do you want to be a low-cost leader in your market niche? Or are you a value-added reseller? Do you add additional value to products in the form of some kind of service charging a higher price? Do you set the price of the products and services you sell, or does the consumer? Whatever pricing model you decide on, you need to make it very clear to the shoppers who come to your site. Consumers do not like surprises. If you promoted your site as the low-price leader, your prices should show it. If you're a boutique shop and charge better-than-average prices, show the value you've added to your products or service. Make it very clear what you charge and why, and be sure it fits the expectations of your site visitors.

Another important point is not to hide your prices. Nothing annoys a shopper more than going through the process of ordering from you, entering their credit card number, and then being told what the total shipped price is. Be sure that you give your shoppers all the information they need to make a buying decision, up front, before they buy. Don't draw the customer into the buying process with low prices and then surprise them after they place their order with exorbitant shipping and handling charges on the order confirmation page. If you want to see a shopper bolt for the door, this is the way to do it.

So how do you inform the shopper of your shipping and handling charges? You can do it in one of two ways.

- Provide an easy-to-find section on your site that lists and easily explains your shipping rates and policies in general and your handling charges.
- Present an order review page to the buyer that lists the price of the product and all applicable shipping and handling charges. Give the buyer the total shipped price before you request his or her credit card number.

We suggest that you do both. That way the shopper fully understands the total amount of the sale before he or she completes the purchase. Don't forget to include any and all applicable taxes in the total of the sale.

Service: How Do You Measure Up?

You've put a lot of effort into building your web store. You've created a good selection of product for your market category and priced your product or service to sell. But that's not enough to earn a customer sale. Customers expect to be serviced, so customer service is a top priority for your website. Because you're not dealing with customers face-to-face, your service policies must instill a sense of trust in your shoppers.

Many current eCommerce companies on the Net today don't understand this simple fact. Consumers expect service. Your web store must deliver it. Good customer service includes

- Email confirmations
- Multiple means of contact
- Support outside business hours
- Guarantees and return policies

Email Confirmations

After a customer clicks the Place My Order button, he or she immediately wonders what will become of his or her order. It's only natural that sending an order into the vastness of cyberspace can cause a certain amount of consternation. You can relieve much of your customer's worries, and avoid frustrations, by sending a series of email confirmations that informs the customer of the status of his or her order right through the sales and shipping process.

As soon as the order is placed, an email confirming that the order was received should be sent to the customer. The Yahoo! store offers this service. The email message should include a complete record of the transaction, including the following information:

- An order number.
- What was ordered.
- Who ordered it.
- Where it will be shipped.
- Total amount of the sale including all shipping and handling costs.
- Customer service contact information in case the customer has a question about the order. Yahoo! store automatically sends an email with all the information cited here except for the customer service contact information. This has to be added by you and you also have the option of additional text in the email confirmation.

Another email message should be sent confirming that the product ordered is in stock and when it will be shipped. A third email message should be sent after the product is actually shipped, containing the name and tracking number of the shipping company that was used. Finally, send an email to your customers after they have received their orders asking them for feedback and even offering them a discount on their next purchase if they buy within the next few weeks. For merchants that use UPS Shipping tools to ship orders in the Yahoo! store Order Manager, an email is sent after processing the order with UPS. The email includes the tracking number, which saves the merchant time cutting and pasting tracking numbers.

Yahoo! store again helps you out here. Yahoo! allows you to create coupons and or discount codes to send to customers if you use their Merchant Standard and Merchant Professional packages.

Provide Multiple Means of Contact

Always provide a number of different ways that a customer can contact your customer service department. There are several ways to do this.

List your customer service email address on your website and include in it all email correspondence with your customer. In addition, tell people where you are located. Include your company's address, telephone number, and fax number on your website.

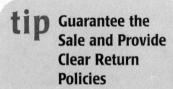

tip **Guarantee the Sale and Provide Clear Return Policies**

One of the best ways to gain customer confidence is to offer them a money-back satisfaction guarantee. As an eBusiness, you should offer a money back guarantee with your products and clearly state your guarantee policy on your website.

List a telephone number for customer service. Let customers know when a live person will answer the telephone. If you use an answering machine, be sure you leave a message that tells the caller when they can expect their call to be returned.

Invest in a toll-free telephone number and list it on your site. Not only is a toll-free number relatively inexpensive, it goes a long way toward building a level of consumer confidence in your business.

Remember that shoppers don't like surprises. Be sure they understand the terms of their purchase before they click the Buy Now button. Tell the shopper under what conditions he or she can return a product. How many days or weeks do they have to decide to return it? Will they get a refund or a credit? Who shows how to use your product or service and gives troubleshooting tips in case customers run into trouble after hours? Be clear and specific and list all details about your return policy on your website.

Remember that it pays to keep all line of communications open with your customers and to provide a quick response to customer emails.

Convenience: Are You Easy to Do Business With?

When a shopper comes to your web store, he's got his credit card in hand and he is ready to buy. So don't let your website get in his way. A web store with a poorly designed navigation structure will frustrate a shopper. Even though you have a great offer, if the shopper can't easily find it and buy it, he'll click off to your competitor and probably will not come back.

A lot of thought must be given to how a shopper can search for products on your site. If you offer a shopper multiple navigation options, it will help her find what she is looking for fast. Have the capability on your site for shoppers to search by

- Product name
- Price
- Product category
- Manufacturer

The more site tools shoppers have to search with, the faster they can get to the products they're looking for, and the faster you'll make a sale.

Web Resource

Offer Live Customer Support—Without the Expense

Want to give live customer support on your site to shoppers? Don't want to spend the money for programming? Then use Yahoo! Instant Messaging at messenger.yahoo.com. Shoppers can download the free desktop application and communicate with you in real-time if they have a question. But, you have to be there for it to work.

But finding a product to buy is only the beginning. Just as important as price selection and service is convenience. How easy is it to navigate through your site? Getting lost in a site is discouraging and will send the shopper away fast if he can't easily find his way through your web store. Good site navigation entails telling your visitor where he is, how he got there, how he can get back, and where he can go next.

If your site navigation is done properly, your shoppers should be able to get to where they want to go in just three mouse clicks (Three Click Rule). Be careful when designing the navigation bar on your site. Graphic links to the different sections of your site are nice and give a professional look to your web store. But also include text links that duplicate your graphic navigation at the bottom of your pages in case your site loads too slowly through a shopper's browser.

Remember that your website should be intuitive to navigate. Your site pages should provide a visual map of how to get from one place to another that says, "Here's where I am. This is what I clicked on to get here. If I click on that, I'll go there next."

Security: How Trustworthy Is Your Site?

Good websites establish trust. Online shoppers can be a very skeptical bunch. They've been trained by the media to expect all kinds of online scams that are waiting to pick their pockets. If up to now you've given them a reason to buy from you, now they have to trust you enough to plunk down their money.

Shoppers are looking for proof that your site is trustworthy to deal with. A good way to do this is join *eTrust* or the *Better Business Bureau (BBB)*. eTrust at www.etrust.com certifies that the personal information you give a site is protected, and the BBB at www.bbbonline.org shows that you abide by the BBB way of doing business.

You build trust in your website in two ways:

- The customer knows his or her credit card number is secure when placing an order on your site. Tell shoppers to your site that their credit card orders are secure. Put that testament right on your home page and on every product page.

- The customer knows that the private personal information he or she gives you is kept personal and private. A good, well written, non-legalese privacy policy should be easily accessible by visitors to your website.

Shoppers are very concerned about using their credit cards to make purchases online. When you build your store on Yahoo!, all credit card transactions are secured on their server. Still, some shoppers just will not place an order online with their credit card, no matter how secure it is. For these types of customers, provide a toll-free telephone number to call in their order to you. Also provide an order form on your site that they can print, fill out, and fax to you.

Privacy Policies

The Internet is a great medium of commerce. With it, you can create new marketing methods, tap new markets, and target potential customers with electronic ease. And it also can get you sued by millions of consumers for violating their privacy!

If you thought spamming consumers with unwanted email was a blight on your company's reputation, consumers are even more upset over the incessant abuse of their personal privacy, not to mention the government investigating the business practices of e-businesses. But companies need to gather a certain amount of information to personalize and better serve their customers. After all, how can you connect with a customer if you know little or nothing about her? There has to be some kind of balance between protecting a consumer's privacy and the need for your business to target and personalize your offers to your customers.

Consumers are sensitive to what's done with their personal information, but it doesn't mean they're against giving it if the circumstances change, including getting something back for the information.

Yahoo! store provides a default Privacy Policy page for your online store, so you are covered there, but you need to read and modify the statement to create your own privacy policy. Finally, make your privacy policy accessible right from your home page (see Figure 3.4).

FIGURE 3.4

The Tube Store combines Yahoo!'s privacy policy with their own.

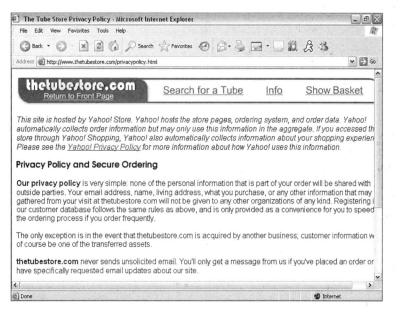

Appendix C provides a worksheet that will help you choose and integrate the different elements of a USP to create a unique selling position for your company. The object of this worksheet is to look at each of the elements and decide which of them, and which parts of them, will help define your USP then integrate them into an effective USP.

Now that you have created your unique selling position, it's time to start planning your Yahoo! Store business. Turn the page and let's get started.

Part II

Planning Your Yahoo! Business

What You'll Learn in This Chapter

- Why you should plan your business
- Choosing a business identity
- Establishing an online domain

CHAPTER

4

Planning to Succeed

So you want to start an online business—any business for that matter. Great! So what's your plan? Your business plan, that is. One of the prime reasons businesses fail is that they don't have plan. Some companies, when asked about their business plan, respond with "I plan to be in business." That's a recipe for trouble. If you haven't written a business plan before you open your business then your business is still in the fantasy stage.

It's not that businesses plan to fail—they fail to plan. No matter what your business, you need to outline your business goals and objectives, costs, revenue assumptions, and marketing plans. In short, a business plan is a practical realistic planning tool for your business that is your roadmap to success and how you'll measure that success.

Why Plan Your Business?

When you say "business plan" to most people, they think of a dry tome used to raise lots of money that's packed with market statistics and financial data with mysterious terms such as "balance sheet," "cash flow," and "profit and loss statements." That's true in most cases. These are necessary parts of most business plans.

But that's only half the story.

Business plans are not only used to acquire funds from investors or bankers, or even obtain company resources. Yes. If you're seeking a capital investment for your business, a sound business plan is necessary for approaching funding sources. If you're in need of company resources for an in-house project then a business plan is necessary for that too.

But a business plan is also a planning tool and a road map to success. It describes your business, acts as your company's résumé, and sets the goals and objectives of your company. One that can organize your thoughts, formalize your intentions, and help sell your idea.

The real power of a business plan is that it forces you to think about the important aspects of your business, whether it's an ongoing operation or a start-up. So, whatever your situation or whatever your objective, writing a business plan will go a long way in helping you succeed.

Briefly, the reasons for writing a business plan include

- Defining a new business venture
- Determining whether your business will make a profit
- Providing an estimate of your start-up costs
- Devising an effective marketing strategy
- Helping you compete in the marketplace
- Anticipating potential problems
- Supporting a loan application
- Raising investment funds
- Expanding a current business or product line
- Defining new goals and objectives for an ongoing business
- Measuring your business performance
- Tracking your growth
- Setting a value on a business for sale or for legal purposes
- Identifying cash flow
- Identifying the competition

- Identifying the necessary human resources

- Identifying the necessary management

- Identifying other resources, office space, desks, computer equipment, telephones, and more

As you can see there are many reasons why you should write a business plan. But there are even more important reasons.

American Express identified a number of ways to achieve business success that are directly connected to writing a business plan. A business plan will force you to think in creative ways about a business that you haven't before. A business plan also forces you to set goals and provides the tools to control the outcome. In short, it can help you translate the raw idea of your company into an actionable plan.

A proper business plan will list your strengths while at the same time prevent you from ignoring your weaknesses. It will make you analyze your competition, build the right team, know your customer, and define your product.

> # caution
>
> ## Why Write That Plan
>
> The consequences of not writing a business plan are many. Dun & Bradstreet tell us that some of the many reasons why 80% of new businesses fail within 5 years are
>
> - Running out of money
> - Failure to make accurate financial projections
> - Lack of adequate funding
> - Poor cash flow
>
> A good solid business plan takes these mistakes into consideration and prepares for them with good financial projections and a realistic sales and distribution strategy.

So, why write a business plan? Because a good, well thought out plan reduces the odds of failure and increases the chances of success. Without a business plan, you leave far too many things to chance.

Major Reasons Why Businesses Fail

Writing a solid business plan can help your business idea come into fruition. But it doesn't guarantee your business will be a success. The following are some of the common mistakes business owners make, and should be avoided AFTER the business plan is written.

- Many companies fail to anticipate the amount of working capital needed to operate a business. Though their financial projections are sound, they run out of money before adequate income from sales hits the bottom line.

- Don't waste working capital when starting a business on frivolous expenses. All your working capital should go for one thing: making sales!

■ Don't be a target of the IRS. Pay your taxes on time. Pay them first before you pay any other expenses. The last thing you need is a lien against your business revenue. It's very tempting to save your tax payments and employee withholdings for last. Don't do it.

■ Remember that most businesses are seasonal. So plan for your industry's highs and lows. Have enough cash on hand for the slow months or diversify your offering to keep your doors open and your business humming along.

'Tis the Season

Something to keep in mind: If you can, the best time to start an online business is near late summer to early fall so you have time to build your store, work out the details, and build site traffic before the holiday rush. Even though you may not offer holiday items, most products can be used as holiday gifts.

If you do run into trouble, here are some tips on how to overcome setbacks in your business.

First, keep the names of a good accountant and attorney handy. And if you do run into problems, seek help and counsel from someone you trust, preferably someone in an industry like yours. They probably have experienced and overcome a problem like that you are now facing at one time or another. Also, don't hide from the problem. Avoiding meetings or phone calls with vendors or whomever else raises a red flag in their minds, and they may interpret it as a problem even more serious than it is. And always keep an upbeat attitude around your employees, no matter what the problems may be. You don't want your best employees getting anxious and looking for work elsewhere.

Look at the problem. If it has to do with cash flow, look for ways to reduce everyday expenses. Cut back on entertainment and travel expenses. If your cash flow is seriously affected, consider cutting back on non-essential employees. If faced with this decision, start by cutting administrative personnel. Keep those that generate the income for your company.

Most importantly, do everything you can to pay your bills on time. Your credit rating is the lifeblood of your business. If you can't make a payment on time, talk to your vendor and work out a plan to deal with the situation. Be proactive and be prepared to offer a payment plan when you call them. Above all, don't make promises you can't keep.

Finally, take a breather to relax and unwind. Take a walk or go to a movie. Then come back with a clear head to tackle the problem.

Some Tips Before You Start

Here are few basic tips to keep in mind even before you start thinking of your plan. These tips are especially useful if you're looking to fund your business plan.

- It pays to take a class or two on running a business while reading up on business plans (try Que's book *Write a Business Plan In No Time*). You should have a general knowledge of the different aspects of a business before you sit down to start your plan. There are many fine courses offered by your local community college, seminars by non-profit organizations, and small business programs offered by the government. Take advantage of these and spend a little time learning the ins and outs of running a business.

- Open a separate business checking account with the name of your business on the checks. Ask your bank about getting a credit card merchant account so you can accept credit cards at your new business. You may be required to provide a deposit to get a merchant account. This is normal for a new business without a track record. So make sure you have the cash for this.

Choosing a Business Identity

A rose by any other name may still be a rose, but what you name your business will affect how the market perceives you. A business name that may seem catchy or cute can often translate into something misleading or ineffective. Because the name of your business is the first interaction a prospective customer has with your business, if they don't understand what you sell, it could lead to lost income.

Here are some ideas to keep in mind to help you avoid that first misleading or even unpleasant impression.

- Don't just make up a name. Creativity in business names is a good thing if not taken too far. Don't butcher the English language to the point where your business name has little or no reflection of what your business does. Sure, companies such as Cingular or Amazon have names that don't match their product or service. But they have the marketing clout to create name recognition. As a small company, unless you are related to Bill Gates in some way, your marketing budget for unique brand recognition will most certainly come up short. Don't make potential customers see your name and ask, "What in the world does that mean?"

■ Don't get cute. Avoid puns or phrases for your business name. This is especially important to avoid if you want to project a highly professional image. "The Shady Lady" may work for a lampshade company but it would definitely draw concern if you were a financial advisor. Also, consider the spelling of your name. Is it easy to spell? Why? It helps when someone is trying to search for your company on the Internet or in the yellow pages. Tricky spellings are hard to look up online or in the phone book. This goes especially for those companies that are looking for top placement in directories. Never put "AAA" or any kind of "A" in your name. We've all seen this at the very front of the phone book. Companies naming themselves "AAA Taxis" is good for top listing, but terrible for customers to remember. One last thing: Keep it short.

■ Name yourself for growth. That unique selling position that you have honed down to a very specific market and product may not make a very good business name. For example, the name "Joe's Music Store" would limit your business. Someday, you might want to add videos and ebooks to your product line. "Joe's Entertainment Outlet" might be a better name to start with. So make sure that your business's name is sufficiently broad enough to encompass whatever direction your business may take. Also, stay away from trendy names. Though tie-dye T-shirts may be making a comeback, it would be better to name your T-shirt store "Al's T-Shirts" than "Al's Groovy Sixties T-shirts."

■ Make sure your name is available. The best place to find out is at your State Corporation Commission. Find the department or agency that handles trade names and do a search on the business name you want to see whether it's available. Also, check the Internet. Do a search on Yahoo.com using the name you chose and see what search results come up.

Establishing Your Online Domain

If you're serious about doing business on the Net you need to register a domain name. A domain name represents your company and is your URL. The letters URL stand for *Uniform Resource Locator*. For example, Amazon's domain name is amazon.com and Wal-Mart's domain name is wal-mart.com. The URL is the site address that appears in the address window of your browser such as www.MyEcommerceSuccess.com. It's the way you find websites on the Net.

A domain name is included with every Yahoo! Merchant Solutions package. Yahoo! will register and renew your domain name for free. If you already have a domain name, you can re-delegate your existing domain and use it with your Merchant Solutions account. Note: This is not a registrar transfer. You will need to continue paying renewal fees with your current registrar. If you do not already have a domain name, you can register for one when you sign-up for a Merchant Solutions account.

When the brick and mortar company Barnes & Noble went online they acquired a domain name. At first they used the long domain name barnes-andnoble.com, then shortened it to bn.com and finally obtained books.com. That, by the way, was some coup. The books.com domain name was the property of another online bookstore. Barnes & Noble wanted it, so they bought the bookstore!

This raises a problem for you. Many of the most popular .com domain names have been taken. You will probably find that someone has already registered your business name or business type. Creating a unique domain name could be quite a challenge. That is, unless you have the deep pockets of a Barnes & Noble to buy an already assigned domain name. The fact is that grabbing a great domain name that reflects your business type or even your business name is getting harder to do. You can also bypass the .com extension and register .net, .org, .us, .info, .name, .biz, .de, .tv, .co.uk, .cc, and .bz, but they are not as popular with users and may cause confusion when they enter your domain name with a .com rather than another extension.

Finally, when choosing a domain name, keep it short and memorable. A long domain name with too many letters or with hyphens is hard to remember. Also, make it easy to spell. Lastly, try to choose a name that relates to your core business or business name.

Where to Start

First, find out whether that nifty domain name you thought up is available. To do that, head over to Yahoo! Small Business at smallbusiness.yahoo.com/merchant/ (see Figure 4.1).

> # caution
>
> ### Register Your Misspelled and Alternative Domain Name
>
> Why lose potential customers because they misspelled your URL? Register the obvious misspellings of your domain name and redirect them back to your site. Also register alternative spellings of your name. To further protect yourself, you might consider registering your domain name not only as a .com, but also as a .net, .org, or even a .tv.

When you arrive at Yahoo! Small Business site, you see a "Find a domain" search box. Type in the domain you would like to use and see whether the name is available.

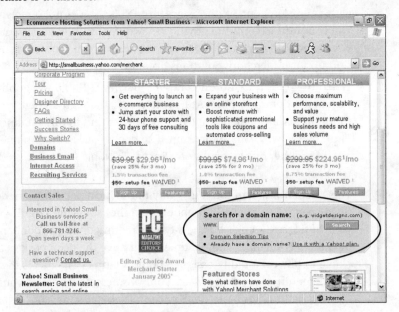

After a quick search, Yahoo! Small Business will tell you whether that domain name is taken or not. Be prepared to try several variations on your domain name until you find one that has not been registered. If the domain name is taken, a list of suggested domain names will be displayed along with the other domain name extensions such as .net, .org, .biz, .info, and .us. Because you are setting up a business on the Net, the extension you will likely use is the .com one. The .org extension is for organizations such as the United Way, and .net is for networks on the Internet. You can search as many names as you like—it's free. After you find the domain name you want and it's available, you can proceed to register the domain name.

Here's the Process to Follow

1. Once you find an available domain name, click the Continue with This Domain button.

2. A page will come up asking which Merchant Solutions plan you would like to choose. Once you select the plan, click the Choose button.

3. Sign in with your Yahoo! ID. If you do not have one, you can create one by clicking the Create One Now link.

4. Yahoo! will then take you through a series of forms asking for your personal, company, and payment information. You can also register for additional domain names and point them to your store. All of your domains can be easily managed in the Domain Control Panel with just one Yahoo! ID. To register for additional domain names, go to smallbusiness.yahoo.com or you can do it in the Domain Control Panel.

Now that you know the reasons to plan your business, have chosen a unique name, and have established a legal identity, it's time to look at the necessary elements of your business plan.

caution

Be Sure You Are the Administrative Contact

You will be asked to name both an administrative and technical contact when you apply for a domain name. It is very important that you name yourself, not an employee, as the administrative contact. The administrative contact is the *only* one who can make changes to your domain registration. Don't be caught having to chase down someone who no longer works for your company to make future changes to your registration.

CHAPTER

5

**What You'll Learn
in This Chapter**

- **Learn how to
  answer the
  essential
  questions of
  a business plan**

- **Learn about
  business plan
  elements**

- **Learn how to
  finance your
  business venture**

Important Elements of a Business Plan

In the previous chapter, we discussed the need to plan your business before you even consider what type of Yahoo! store you want to establish. And the best way to plan your business is to create a business plan. Now, if you are starting a Yahoo! store as a hobby or to prove out a business idea, you probably don't need to put together a detailed business plan, but you should at least document the minimum elements necessary to make your business endeavor a success. Who knows, there are more than enough examples of a hobby or wild idea turning into a multimillion dollar business down the line.

Now if you're a one- or two-person home business or a small neighborhood business with one or two employees, you don't have to write a full-blown 20–40 page business plan complete with financials. But there are important elements of any business plan that you should consider and create. A good resource for business plan writing that covers more material than this chapter allows is *Write a Business Plan In No Time*. Also, you can find more valuable information on business plans on the Yahoo! Small Business site at smallbusiness.yahoo.com/resources/ under "Business Plans."

At a minimum, your plan must clearly communicate who you are, what you do, what your product or service is, what consumer or business need it solves, how you plan to implement your business, what markets you will service, and how much money or how many resources you will need to execute your plan.

So let's get started.

Answering the Essential Questions

Like in life, we all ask essential questions. A business plan is no different. They are

- **Who**: "Who" is your business?
- **What**: What does it sell?
- **Why**: Why is it a business? What need does it solve?
- **When**: What is the implementation plan?
- **Where**: Where is your business and what markets/customers will it service?
- **How**: How will you market your business?
- **How Much**: How much money will you need to get your business started and running?

Who: Who Is Your Business?

You have to be clear on who you are in your business plan. Why? Well, for example, if you're going to seek funding for your business idea, investors and bankers will surely want to know who they are dealing with. They will want to know about your experience, your skills, and your role in the business you chose. In addition, they will want to know who will supply the business experience and expertise you may lack and your plans on how to acquire that extra talent.

You should also know something about yourself. Do you feel that you have what it takes to start and run a new business? Are you willing and able to put in the long hours and hard work a new enterprise entails? Are you financially able to survive through the tough start up months? And most important of all, do you have the traits of an entrepreneur?

Web Resource

Resources for the Entrepreneur

There are many resources on the Internet that can assist entrepreneurs. A good one is entrepreneur.com. This website is packed with actionable information that will help you start and grow your business. You'll find articles and resources on starting a business, running a home office, money and finance, eCommerce, and technology.

Finally, who is your business? What will your legal structure be? Is it a sole proprietorship? A partnership? A corporation?

What: What Does It Sell?

The purpose of a business is to sell something. It may be a product or a service, or it may sell information. In any case, your business plan must be able to explain in detail what kind of product or service you plan to sell. What is it? What makes it unique? How does it compare with your competition? Do they dominate your market niche? If so, can a newcomer break into the market? How do you plan to compete? Do you have a competitive advantage? What is it? Is your product as good as your competition? Better? Why? What is your USP?

You must also look ahead. Once you're established in the marketplace, can a new company easily undercut your prices or your earnings with a newer product or service? Do you have a barrier to competition? If so, what is it?

Why: Why Is It a Business? What Need Does It Solve?

We've all heard the joke about the dumb salesman trying to sell refrigerators to Eskimos. As it turns out, it's not dumb at all. Refrigerators serve a real purpose in frigidly cold weather. They keep the food from freezing solid. This is an example of finding a need and meeting it. What you sell must do the same thing.

You have to clearly explain how your product meets a consumer need. To do that, you have to identify your target customers (demographics), and explain how your product or service will meet their needs. Who are you targeting? Consumers? Retailers? Wholesalers? The government? Is your product practical? Will it fill a need? What need?

You also need to identify where or how you will be acquiring your products. Who are your suppliers? And who are your backup suppliers if your primary ones fail to deliver? If you're manufacturing your own product, who is supplying your parts?

And finally, where will your business be located? What physical space will be necessary? Office space? Retail space? Warehouse space? A combination of some sort? Are you starting a home-based business? If so, do you have space in your home? Where will you locate it? What about your community's CC&Rs (conveniences, conditions, and restrictions)? Their conditions and restrictions on what you can use your home for? Will they allow for a home business such as yours?

When: What Is the Implementation Plan?

A business plan will do you little good if you don't have a strategy to implement it. Things to consider in your plan are how many months of zero revenue will be needed to start up your business? Do you have a phased plan for development complete with what you wish to accomplish, by when, including what must take place before each phase happens? What are your major decision points? What milestones do you want to hit and by when? What actions are needed to meet those milestones?

In summary, an implementation plan lays out your company's objectives, the tasks or actions necessary to reach those objectives, a timescale of events or actions, and a way to monitor your progress.

Where: Where Is Your Business and What Markets/ Customers Will It Service?

Whether there is a market for your product or service is just as important as the product or service itself. The business landscape is littered with companies who thought they had a great product or service idea, brought it to market, and discovered few people or no one was interested in buying it. Market research will tell you whether or not there is a market for your product or service.

Who will buy your product? What are their demographics? Do they shop online? What online areas do they frequent? Back up your findings with real data from private, public, or government sources such as census information, databases, and industry information. What is the potential size of your market? How big a piece of the market can you garnish for your business? How do you feel you can serve this market? Why?

If you've done your research well, you will have a very good idea of the size of your market, the makeup of its consumers, and the important information you will need to create your marketing plan.

How: How Will You Market Your Business and Your Product or Service?

Marketing your company and what it sells is the cornerstone of a successful marketing plan. All is for naught if you can't actually sell the product or service your company offers. To do that you will need to create a demand for what you sell. Demand is created through advertising, publicity, and promotional programs.

What are your plans for marketing your business? Are they realistic and based upon your proposed marketing budget in your financials? What is your overall marketing strategy? How will your choice of marketing vehicles help you reach your target market? What advertising media will you use? TV? Radio? The Internet? Some combination of them? Will you use direct mails or telemarketing to reach potential customers? How will you use public relations in your marketing mix? Will trade shows, seminars, and workshops also be included in your marketing plan? How will you use them? Where and when?

How your business plan answers these questions is critical to the success of your company.

How Much: How Much Money Will You Need to Get Your Business Started and Running?

Money and resources are the lifeblood of any business. So, you'll need to know how much you need to breathe life into yours.

What is your source of funds and/or resources? Will you need financing? What kind? SBA loan (Small Business Association)? Equity? Debt? A combination of both? How much will your business need to reach break even? How much will you need to meet your sales and revenue projections? If it's a start up, how will you compensate yourself? What are the personal resources that you'll contribute to the business? If you're seeking a loan from a bank, your friendly banker will want to know what kind of financial risk you're personally taking.

What about human resources? Who will you need to hire and how much will they cost? What technical resources will you need? Where will you buy them? How much will they cost? Will you need some special business insurance? What is it? What will it cost?

A lot of questions? Yes. But every one is important and should be answered whether you are a home or small business. And you answer these questions in the elements of your business plan.

Business Plan Elements

"Parts is parts" the saying goes. Not so when writing a business plan. The structure of a business plan is not random. It has a logical progression of thought. The marketing plan comes after the information on your product or service but before your implementation and financial information. As for the other parts, the order they appear in your plan depends upon the best way you feel you can communicate and sell your business concept.

Certain parts of a standard business plan may not apply to your business. For instance, if you're going to sell directly to the public as a retailer then your plan will need to detail where and how you will purchase your products, but your distribution or sales strategy will be pretty basic. On the other hand, if you're manufacturing a product to sell then your plan will focus more on its distribution strategy. All plans should answer two basic questions:

- Is this a product or service that people will buy?
- Are you the right person to make your idea a success?

So let's look at the basic elements that make up a business plan. They are

- Executive Summary
- Company Mission and Objectives
- Overview of Your Company
- Description of Your Product or Service
- Marketplace
- Marketing Strategy
- Competition
- Implementation Plan
- Capital Requirements

The **Executive Summary** is probably the most important section of your plan. Why? Because it's the first thing that is read *but* the last thing you write. That's because it is a short summary of all the most important parts of your business plan, meant to sell your idea to the reader. If you can grab their interest then they will be more likely to read the details of your plan.

Since it is a summary, you have to wait until you've written all the parts of your business plan before you write the Executive Summary.

But remember, an Executive Summary is just that—a *summary*, not a foreword. In effect, it's your entire plan in a nutshell, your elevator pitch.

The sections of your plan that deal with your company itself are the Company Mission and Objectives and Company Overview sections.

The **Company Mission and Objective** section details your company mission and vision statements. It describes what your business will do and why. It also lays out a vision of your company and where it wants to be in the future. The **Company Overview** provides a description of your company—start up, existing company, legal form, and so on—and its goals and objectives.

The focus of what you intend to sell and how you will sell it is in the **Product or Service Description** section of your plan. Here you will not only describe what you intend to sell but also what human needs it fulfills. In other words, this section will describe your product and service in detail, and explain your unique selling position (USP).

Hand in hand with your product or service description is an analysis of the **Marketplace** you will sell within and the **Marketing Strategy** you will use to market your product or service.

Finally, the section of **Distribution Channels** will explain the distribution or sales channels you will use to sell your product through. In our case, the Internet through a Yahoo! store.

A business plan is not only a selling document but a planning one too. Plan your work and work your plan. It represents a roadmap that your company plans to follow to implement your business idea and forces you to look closely enough at all of the details to really understand your own business and how it will unfold. That's the purpose of the **Implementation Plan**. This plan describes step by step how you plan to carry out your business plan.

The last section of your business plan would deal with money and resources. It will list the **Capital Requirements** you will need to launch and operate your company to break even. And speaking of capital requirements, you should spend some time evaluating your funding needs and where the funds you need to launch your new business venture online will come from.

A good place to create a short but effective business plan for your part-time home business is at the website of the *Wall Street Journal*. It offers a free mini-plan wizard at wsj.miniplan.com.

Once you have your business plan written, it's time set up the necessary accounts for your business. In the next chapter we will cover how to find and choose an ISP (Internet service provider), how to set a shipping center and accounts, and how to set up a credit card merchant account.

Setting Up Your Business Accounts

You've set up your back office, chosen your business identity, and lined up the financial resources you need to start your eBusiness. Are you ready to open your doors? No. Not quite yet. You still have to set up your business accounts.

These consist of choosing an Internet service provider (ISP) that will give you access to the Internet, choosing who will host your online storefront, setting up a shipping center and the necessary shipping accounts, record-keeping system, and merchant account to accept credit cards.

That's a lot to do, so let's get started.

Boarding the Information Highway

In order to access the Yahoo! store technology and the Internet itself, you will need to have an account at an Internet service provider. These companies allow you to access the Internet from your computer. Basically, there are two ways to board the information highway, dial-up or broadband. Your choice will mostly depend on how fast you want web pages to load when being viewed and how much you want to spend per month. Your choice might also be limited to the area of the country you live in.

Web Resource	**ISP buying Guide**

ISP buying Guide

CNET at http://reviews.cnet.com/ISP_buying_guide/4520-7606_7-728424-1.html has a very useful ISP buyers' guide on their site. It helps you can answer the following questions:

- What kind of ISP is right for me?
- What kind of access is available?
- What services and features should I expect?
- What potential problems should I watch for?

A dial-up connection is very slow (maximum 56.6 kilobits per second). It requires a phone line and your computer modem. You will need to dial in every time you want to connect to the Internet. While connected, you will not be able to use your phone because the Internet connection is using your phone line. If you need to use the phone while connected to the Internet, you can choose to install a second phone line or just use your cell phone.

There are two basic types of broadband connection: cable modem and DSL. A broadband connection can be 10 times or more faster than a dial-up connection. Speed will vary depending on the type of broadband connection you choose and whether the connection is shared among other users. Let's take a look at each one.

Broadband

High-speed *cable modem* Internet service is provided by your cable company. It's a direct connection and uses the same line as your cable TV. Unlike dial-up, you don't have to wait to connect and it will free up your telephone line. Cable modems have the capability of delivering speeds of 4–5 megabits per second. In reality, this will vary depending on the number of subscribers in your area who are using the network. Using a cable modem will require you to purchase or lease a cable modem, pay for an installation fee if you do not know how to install it yourself, and acquire an Ethernet card if your computer does not already have one.

Using a cable modem along with a router will allow multiple computers in your house to access the Internet without paying extra. Most cable companies offer discounted packages if you subscribe to their other services. Check with your local cable provider for special offers.

DSL

Another high-speed internet alternative is *DSL (Digital Subscriber Line)*. DSL uses the data portion of the phone line that your telephone voice line does not use. With DSL, you can connect to the Internet and use the telephone simultaneously. Most DSL providers will include the DSL modem with your service. Unlike with cable modems, DSL customers do not share bandwidth with other subscribers in the area. Download speeds will vary by provider. Contact your DSL provider to find out downstream and upstream speeds.

So which method is right for you?

Your Internet connection options will depend on your budget, location, and needs. If you are serious about starting an online business, it's highly recommended that you get a broadband connection. Dial-up is very slow and it's best if you spend your time developing and marketing your store and not waiting for your store pages to download and upload.

Finding an ISP

For cable modem service, contact your local cable company to see if they provide high-speed Internet access at your location. For DSL, contact SBC Yahoo! DSL at www.sbc.com. SBC Yahoo! DSL has introductory rates starting at $16.95. You can check the SBC Yahoo! DSL website to see if the service is offered in your area.

If SBC Yahoo! DSL is not provided in your area, you can find others with pricing for your state at www.myispfinder.org (see Figure 6.1).

When Your Internet Service Provider Doesn't Provide Service

Your business is cruising along, prospects are being pitched, sales are coming in, orders are going out. You're a self-made online success. Life is good. Then one day, out of the blue, you cannot connect to the Internet to retrieve orders, you are not able to download your customer service emails, and you cannot get to your website.

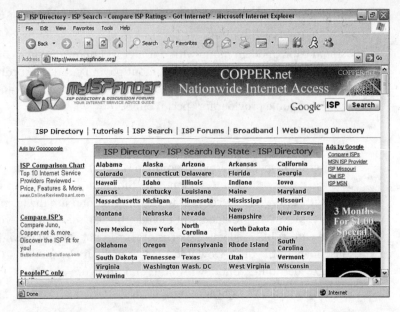

You're in doo-doo city because your ISP just went belly-up! Now what do you do?

If you're lucky, you may get a short but polite email from your ISP stating, in so many words, that they have succumbed and will cease operations shortly. This may give you some time to scramble and hunt down a quick and temporary way to access your online business. But as the U.S. Marines say, it's better to "Be prepared."

So, you "make hay when the sun shines" and prepare for the unthinkable right now.

So, here are some things to do to prepare for the unthinkable.

First, keep that analog modem you have in your machine or in a handy place for retrieval. If your ISP goes bye-bye, you're going to need it as a temporary measure to come online again. Sign up for a free ISP or low-cost service such as Juno. You know those CDs you regularly receive in the mail from AOL, MSN, and other ISPs? Stop using them as coasters and put one aside for emergencies. Any of these large ISPs will enable you to get back online in a hurry if your current connection goes down. In fact, keep a few around as backup. Or sign up now for a low-cost ISP. You should sign up for one of them and make your monthly payments like you would an insurance premium. CNET at www.cnet.com/internet/0-3762-8-6719328-1.html does a good job of reviewing and recommending the four top bargain ISPs. Most of these cheap ISPs limit the time you spend online and force you to look at banner ads, but if you're getting something for next to nothing, you can expect to put up with a few inconveniences.

Second, look for warning signs that your ISP might show up on the dead list. If you're using a prominent, publicly traded ISP, read news headlines and track the company's stock prices. Bad headlines and dropping prices could mean trouble ahead. For warning signs on privately held ISPs, keep tabs on their service level. For example, if reaching someone in customer service is like getting blood from a stone, or your email or Net connection goes up and down like a yo-yo, then your ISP may be headed for trouble. Another warning sign is if your ISP starts asking you to pay by check or cash and not by credit card.

Third, get intelligence from the Net community. Watch for consumer alerts on the website of your local Better Business Bureau. Also, watch for complaints and warnings posted on sites such as Slashdot at www.slashdot.org and Broadband Reports at www.dslreports.com (see Figure 6.2), which serve as community forums for ISP customers.

FIGURE 6.2

Broadband Reports gives users a chance to speak their mind about the ISP they use.

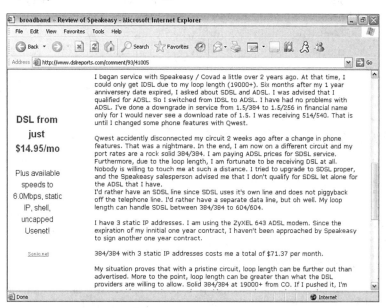

Finally, don't wait! Prepare for the worst now. You may not have the time if your Internet service provider...doesn't. Like the old sage said, "An ounce of prevention is worth a pound of cure."

Setting Up Your Email Account

Yahoo! Mail offers a free email account. You can sign up for one at mail.yahoo.com. Yahoo! Mail comes with virus protection; anti-spam guard; Yahoo! Photo, which allows you to store unlimited photos; and you can also receive alerts on your phone when new mail arrives. Since Yahoo! Mail is web based, you can access your email from another computer or device with an Internet connection. It's recommended that you create an account with Yahoo! because it can also be your account ID to access your Yahoo! store.

Yahoo! Mail Business Edition comes with every Merchant Solutions account. You can also use an email address with your domain name, such as your-name@yourdomain.com. Using an email address with your domain name will help you brand your website. Each account includes up to 100 individual email accounts. Unlike other email programs, each email account has the capability to send and receive large file attachments up to 10 megabits. Not only can you set up an email POP account and use your preferred email client such as Outlook or Outlook Express, but you can also set up a webmail account to send and receive email via any web browser like through Yahoo! Mail. This comes in handy when you are away from your personal computer and still need to be in touch with your customers and receive orders.

In Chapter 10, "Setting Up Your Yahoo Store Order Settings," you will learn how to set up your email accounts using the email control panel.

Setting Up Your Shipping Center

We spoke earlier about what was required to set up your office for business. You might call the area where you do all your online business your "front office." So let's take some time and talk about your back office. This is the area where you'll pack and ship your orders. You'll also need to set up a separate area near your shipping center for inventory storage.

Designating the Space

If selling merchandise is your business, the size of the items you sell will dictate the size of the inventory storage and shipping space you'll need. The smaller the items, the less space you will need, and vice versa. Whatever the size of the space, make sure it's dedicated to shipping only. That way you will always have a permanent shipping center set up and ready go.

Make sure your shipping center has enough space for a large flat table to pack your items, storage space for your packing supplies, and a staging area to temporarily store your packages that are ready to be picked up by your shipping company.

Where do you find such a space? Since you're operating your business from home, you'll have to find a space large enough in your house. Your garage is good place to start, and if you have a basement in your home, that's another fine place to set up your shipping center. Wherever you choose, the space must be large enough to accommodate your packaging activities and staging area.

Essential Supplies

Your shipping center needs space not only for packaging your orders, but to store your shipping supplies. You should have enough shipping supplies on hand for at least a week of orders. Here's a list of the basic shipping supplies you will need.

- Shipping labels
- Return address labels (your return address can be incorporated into your shipping label)
- Bubble wrap
- Styrofoam packing peanuts
- Scissors
- Box cutter
- Tape (Clear tape is recommended. That way you can use it to tape over the shipping label to make it somewhat waterproof.)
- Black magic marker
- Postal scale
- Forms, rate lists, and other shipping supplies provided by your shipping service

What about shipping boxes? There's some good news there. Most shipping companies such as FedEx will supply you with an assortment of different size boxes if you use their shipping service. But you should also carry larger boxes than they supply to accommodate any size order.

Web Resource

Where to Find Shipping Supplies

Check out these websites for shipping supplies:

- BubbleFAST at www.bubblefast.com
- eSupplyStore at www.esupplystore.com

Managing Your Inventory

If you're setting up a small home business, you will be faced with the challenge of finding a place to store your inventory. If your items are small, you shouldn't have any problem finding space. But if the products you sell are bigger than a breadbox, you have a space challenge.

Here are some suggestions:

- Your garage
- Your basement
- A spare room
- A closet

If you can't find the space in your home then look to the outside. Or perhaps you have a storage shed outside your home. You can always rent one of those storage bins or even a small warehouse space. Whatever you choose, make sure it's convenient and close to where you process your orders.

Choosing Your Shipping Method

You have a number of different methods to choose from to ship your orders. Each requires that you set up an account with the shipping company you choose. Consider which options your customers would like to use and whether they're viable for business. Don't base your decision on just whether its convenient for you. Many shoppers abandon orders after seeing shipping costs, so anything you can do to make rates cheap(er), fast(er), and accurate will cut down on customer contacts, complaints, and most importantly, increase conversion rates and repeat shoppers.

The most popular shipping services include the U.S. Post Office (USPS) and the different types of mail they offer—such as regular mail, Express Mail, Priority Mail, and so on—and Federal Express (FedEx) and United Parcel Service (UPS) who offer next day, second day, and ground services. Let's take a look at each one and the service they offer.

USPS

The United States Postal Service is the granddaddy of all shipping services. They have managed to compete with the johnny-come-latelies such as FedEx and UPS and offer next day and priority delivery services.

- **Express Mail**—This is USPS version of FedEx and UPS guaranteed next day delivery. Merchandise is automatically insured up to $100.

■ **Priority Mail**—This type of delivery is in the two to three day range. The good news is that USPS supplies you with free Priority Mail boxes and is not as expensive to use as Express Mail.

■ **Parcel Post**—Though inexpensive compared to Express Mail and Priority Mail, it can take up to a week or more for a package to reach its destination.

> **tip Got Media? Send It Cheap.**
>
> The USPS has a shipping rate called Media Mail. If you are selling and shipping different types of media items including CDs, DVDs, video tapes, and any kind of printed media such as books and magazines, this rate can save you money. It used to be called "book rate" and the rates are much lower than Priority Mail and delivery times range between First Class delivery and Parcel Post, typically less than a week.

You can find out more about the shipping services of USPS at www.usps.com. You can also view their domestic calculator at www.postcalc.usps.gov to calculate postage for all levels of service. Also, USPS has a great online mail label service called Endicia, where you enter the address and weight and print the labels right from your PC.

UPS

UPS is a good service if you are shipping large packages that the U.S. Postal Service will not accept. The USPS does have a size and weight limit, but UPS does not. UPS offers several different shipping options including Standard Ground, Next Day Air, and Second Day Air. They also have a service called Next Day Air Saver. It's an affordable delivery option for those important shipments that require next-business-day delivery, but doesn't have to be there in the morning. UPS also has "print the labels right from the PC." All you do is print and tape it on the box. Then just drop it off at the nearest UPS or Mail Boxes Etc. store.

They are a bit pricey on small packages but the service of choice for large and heavier ones. You will have to set up an account with them and they will supply you with the necessary shipping forms.

UPS Online Tools is also integrated with Yahoo! Merchant Solutions at no extra cost. With UPS Online Tools, you can process shipments without leaving your store manager, auto-insert tracking numbers into orders, and auto-populate shipping labels. Also, merchants can print shipping UPS labels with a standard printer. With the UPS Online Tools module that plugs into the checkout pages, you can do the following: display official UPS services selected for use by you; display real-time rates from UPS; use the Time in Transit module to display the length of time each shipping method will take; and use UPS Address Verification to catch any inputs errors from shoppers.

Learn more about UPS Online Tools at promotions.yahoo.com/ups/static/ merchant_center.html. You can also establish an account in the Shipping Manager control panel in your store. Establishing an account through the Shipping Manager will ensure that the UPS Online Tools is integrated with your store.

FedEx

FedEx is most probably the fastest shipping service but you pay for that result. Their rates are higher than USPS and can be higher than UPS.

They offer guaranteed overnight, second day, and ground shipping. You will need to set up an account with FedEx to ship packages with them. Once you've signed up, they will provide you with the necessary shipping forms, and if you have many packages to ship at a time, they will pick up at your home office. One advantage, as we said before, is that FedEx will supply you with an assortment of free shipping boxes.

For more information on FedEx, go to their website at www.fedex.com and establish an account there. You also access their domestic rate calculator at fedex.com/us/rates.

Free Info   Download the free informative article entitled "A World of Shopkeepers" at www.MyEcommerceSuccess.com.

Setting Up Your Merchant Account

A merchant account is required before you can open up for business. This is in addition to opening a Yahoo! Merchant Solutions account. Yahoo! cannot process online credit card orders without a merchant account. The merchant account provider is the agent that acts on behalf of the merchant to facilitate credit card transactions between the issuing bank of the buyer and the merchant.

For you to accept credit cards and have the customer's card charged to your account, thereby collecting your money, you must establish a merchant account at a bank. Establishing a credit card merchant account can be tricky and fraught with problems if you don't do it right. In addition, there are thousands of what are called *field agents* who aggressively recruit small merchants into merchant account programs that sound great on the surface but have hidden costs that can drive up the costs of accepting credit cards. More of that later.

The Yahoo! shopping cart (or the shopping basket) is only one of two parts of a shopping cart. The second part is the cash register. The shopping cart keeps track of and tallies the order; the cash register records, processes, and charges the customer's credit card.

Here's how it works.

The customer's credit card information is transmitted through a Secure Socket Layer (SSL) to Yahoo!. After your customer has entered his credit card information into Yahoo!'s shopping cart order form and clicked **Send Order**, that information is sent from their SSL server to Yahoo!'s credit card processing server, or what's called the *payment gateway*. The payment gateway, or credit card processing agent, performs a very important function. The agent is responsible for verifying the customer's credit card information and confirming that there are sufficient funds in the customer's account to cover a purchase.

The payment gateway then passes this information on to the bank where you have your merchant account, which then contacts the customer's credit card issuer that approves or denies credit. This notice is then passed back down the chain to the payment gateway and then to you.

Setting Up a Merchant Account

With Yahoo!'s Merchant Solutions packages, you can choose to apply for Paymentech (paymentech.com), Yahoo! Merchant Solutions's preferred provider, or any other compatible First Data Merchant Services (FDMS) Nashville platform merchant account (fdms.com). Yahoo! Store uses FDMS Nashville platform as a payment gateway to process transactions from your store with your merchant account.

In Chapter 10, we will show you how to apply for a merchant account with

> ## caution
>
> ### What's a Payment Gateway?
>
> The payment gateway only verifies that a credit card is valid and that the cardholder has enough credit in his account to purchase the product he selected. A payment gateway is just an agent and does not verify that the card is stolen or being used by someone other than the cardholder.

> ## caution
>
> ### Being Disapproved for a Merchant Account?
>
> Some merchants will not be approved for a merchant account. Some of the reasons may be due to poor credit rating or the website not being finished. Some merchant account providers will verify your website before approving your merchant account. If you are disapproved for a merchant account due to credit rating, you may want to look into using PayPal.

Paymentech and how to integrate your own FDMS Nashville platform compatible merchant account with your store.

If you chose to use a merchant account provided by your own bank or another solution provider, you must be very careful when choosing a merchant account. If you choose incorrectly, the costs incurred on each and every credit card sale you make could dramatically affect your bottom line. So, keep these possible fees in mind when evaluating which bank to use to process your credit cards. If your bank can't compete, move your business checking account.

Certain fees are associated with setting up a merchant account and processing customers' credit cards. It's not done for free. If you don't know what the required fees are, you can make a mistake that will cost you extra money on each and every credit card sale you make.

So, what's it going to cost?

First, there's the merchant account setup fee. This can run from a few hundred to a thousand dollars. Most merchant account setup fees are in the $400–$600 range.

The second fee is what's called the *discount rate*. Using the word "discount" makes it sound like you're getting a deal, right? You aren't. This is the percentage of the sale that your merchant bank will charge you on each credit card charge. For example, if your customer has purchased $100 in merchandise from you and you're going to charge his card $100, you will have to pay your merchant bank a percentage of that sale to process the customer's credit card.

This percentage can range between 2% and 3% for Visa, MasterCard, and Discover and 3% to 5% for American Express. So if your discount rate for a Visa card is 2%, your Merchant Bank will take 2%—or $2 of that $100 customer purchase—and deposit the remainder in your bank account. And by the way, that percentage is on top of the total credit card charge, including shipping and handling.

The third fee a merchant bank might charge you is a *transaction fee*. This fee is in addition to the discount fee and is the charge that your merchant bank assesses to process the credit card sale. Expect to pay between $0.25 and $0.70 per transaction.

And the fees don't stop there.

Your merchant bank might require you to pay a monthly statement fee on top of all the other fees. Statement fees range between $10 to $15 a month. You also might be charged a minimum processing fee of up to $25 a month. This fee is usually waived if your credit card sales meet your merchant bank's minimum monthly credit card sales.

A *charge-back* is what your bank does when they reverse a charge on your customer's credit card. Reasons for this include fraudulent or unauthorized use of the customer's credit card or simple dissatisfaction with your product if you've refused to take back the product and issue a credit to their account. You can reduce the threat of charge-backs by providing good customer service and offering a 100% customer satisfaction guarantee. There is no reason why you shouldn't offer such a guarantee unless the products you sell are so personalized that you could not resell them.

Free Info   Download the free informative article entitled "A Penny Saved Is a Penny Earned: Preventing Online Fraud" at www.MyEcomerceSuccess.com.

There also might be a holdback for charge-backs. Your bank might want to hold a sizable deposit against your sales to cover any charge-backs that you incur.

Do you have to pay all these fees?

That depends on your bank and the relationship you have with them. The credit card business is very competitive and now that eCommerce is the hottest thing in business, many banks are aggressively lowering and even eliminating fees to attract eBusinesses. There are hundreds of credit card programs available to eTailers today and if you do your research, you'll find merchant banks that will not charge statement fees, minimum monthly processing fees, or even setup fees. But you have to take the time and make the effort to look around.

Web Resource   ## Merchant Services Companies

Here are some companies that specialize in merchant accounts for online merchants and are First Data Merchant Services (FDMS) compatible.

- 1st American Card Service—www.1stamericancardservice.com
- Card Service International—www.cardservice.com
- Chase Merchant Services—www.chasemerchantservices.com
- Wells Fargo Merchant Services—www.wellsfargo.com
- First Bank—www.fbol.com
- Bank of Hawaii—www.boh.com
- Express Merchant Processing Solutions—www.empsebiz.com
- First Interstate Bank—www.firstinterstatebank.com

Using PayPal

With the new integration of PayPal, merchants now can use PayPal with
Checkout Manager. Merchants can open for business with just a PayPal
account or use PayPal in addition to a merchant account. Before, merchants
were required to have a merchant account (online or offline) in order to open
for business. With PayPal, there is no monthly fee or setup fee, and transaction fees range from 1.9% to 2.9% depending on the number of transactions
per month. Also with 78 million registered PayPal accounts around the world,
you have a huge group of potential new customers. For more information
about using PayPal with your Yahoo! store, go to
smallbusiness.yahoo.com/merchant/paypal.php.

And don't be afraid to push these providers into a bidding war. With a little
research and planning, getting a merchant account can be painless and inexpensive. It also can protect you from less-reputable providers who know they
can make a quick buck off a web merchant who's new to the game of accepting credit cards.

Okay. You have your business accounts set up and you're ready for the next
step. In the next chapter we'll discuss the tools of the trade needed to build
your Yahoo! store.

Part III

Setting Up Your Yahoo! Store

Tools of the Trade

Setting up an online store is similar to establishing a store in the physical world. That is, you have to build it. But instead of bricks and mortar and hammers and nails, you will be using bits and bytes and computer hardware and software.

Choosing and having the correct tools is important to building a successful Yahoo! store. Though Yahoo! store will provide you with all the online templates you need to build your online storefront, you have to have the necessary tools to utilize Yahoo!'s store-building technology. But not to worry…this chapter will provide you a list of items that you will need to acquire.

Basic Tools–
Hardware Requirements

Job one in building your Yahoo! store is having the necessary computer hardware to run the programs to access the Yahoo! store building site. Starting out with the proper type of computer system will make your life much easier when working with the store templates and other store building tools that Yahoo! provides.

caution

Check It Out
Before You Buy

Before you purchase software, make sure you consult with the software provider to verify whether the computer you are using meets the system requirements.

Having a reliable computer is essential to your business. It's even more so when creating an online storefront. With the continuous price cuts in personal computers, you can purchase a system today that will most likely meet your hardware requirements for as little as $299. Though this kind of system is attractive for the price, we would recommend that you spend a little extra for more computing power. With software requiring more and more horsepower these days, a more advanced computer will be more likely to accommodate all your future system requirements.

Although there are no system requirements for using Yahoo! Store Editor, there will be system requirements for some of the other software that you may want to use to help build or market your store. The following is a list of system requirements that will meet the needs of most of the software requirements in this chapter.

- Operating system: Windows Me/XP/2000
- Processor: 1.5GHz Pentium III or Athlon Processor
- Memory: 256MB
- Disk Space: 40GB

Yahoo Talk   **Yahoo! Store Editor**

Store Editor is Yahoo!'s online tool for building your store. It's great for those who do not know HTML and want to quickly get their site up and running.

If you're not familiar with computer terminology, an operating system, or OS, is the software program that is used to control all other software programs. It's the software that first comes up when you start your computer and allows your other programs to run. For the PC, an example of an OS is Windows Me, XP, or 2000. The CPU, or central processing unit, is the brain of the computer. That's the computer chip inside your desktop or laptop computer that interprets and computes instructions.

Bill Gates or Microsoft once said that 64K was more than enough RAM you need for a computer. Boy, was he wrong. RAM, or random access memory, is the computer's memory that your software programs use to temporarily store data for rapid access. The more RAM you have, the more software programs you can run simultaneously. Having more memory will also speed up the processing time and your Internet online activity. As the old saying goes, you can never have too much RAM!

Finally, there's disk space. Disk space is the amount of data your computer can store on your hard drive. The greater the disk space, the more software programs you can install and the more data files you can have on your computer. Today's hard drives will provide you with more than enough space to store your programs and data.

Oops! I Lost My Data!

Although Yahoo! backs up all your store data and website files, it's essential to back up your computer files. You may have email, accounting data, customer contact, product images, software programs, and invoices that may be crucial to your business. Having a hard drive crash or a virus may set you back days to recover if it can be recovered. Companies have gone out of business because of computer system crashes. Some companies were not even able to recover invoices to bill customers.

To avoid such disasters and speed up recovery time, it is a great idea to have a backup system and schedule in place. Backup software such as Ghost by Symantec (www.symantic.com) along with an external hard drive can be a great solution. You can even schedule the software to perform automatic routine backups of your computer. Ghost will allow you to quickly restore individual files, folders, or the entire hard drive.

Yahoo Talk   ### Yahoo! Backup

Does Yahoo! backup my data in case of emergencies?

All website online store data is backed up in real-time in their main data center. The same data is also copied and stored to another data center located in another geographical site for added protection.

Basic Tools: Software Requirements

The best hardware for running a business is useless without the right software. Having the right software for the right job will not only help you save time but also streamline your business tasks. There are many different computer programs on the market today that can meet your software requirements, but we recommend you stick with the Microsoft suite of software programs called Microsoft Office (www.microsoft.com).

Microsoft Office comes with a suite of applications that will be a great help to your online business. The standard edition includes Word, PowerPoint, Outlook, and Excel. The Professional Edition comes with everything from the standard edition plus Access and Publisher. Let's look at them one at time and see why they are good tools for building and maintaining a Yahoo! store.

- **MS Word**—Word is the best selling word processing software program used to create text documents. It's a great program for producing customer invoices and letters.

- **MS PowerPoint**—Planning on making a business presentation? PowerPoint is a professional presentation software program that will also allow you to add video and audio, and even collaborate online. You can also make your PowerPoint presentation available on your store website.

- **MS Outlook**—Outlook is an email client that also manages your important contacts, schedules, tasks, and notes. You can also have an email confirmation of every order sent immediately to this email client.

- **MS Excel**—Excel is a spreadsheet application that will allow you to create custom formulas for instant calculations. You can export your orders from your Yahoo! store into Excel for easy viewing and processing. You can also perform a database upload to add new products or update product info with a .csv file using Excel.

- **MS Access**—Want to create your own database and custom reports for your business? Access is a relational database application that you can use to export your customer orders and import them into Access. You can also create advanced reports to see other trends and statistics of your business.

- **MS Publisher**—Man does not live by online alone. You may want to create flyers to advertise sales or make an announcement. So, why not design a professional-looking flyer? Publisher will allow you to create professional-looking promotional material and print it using any regular printer. You can even make your publications available to customers who visit your online store.

Besides the integrated suite of software products of Microsoft Office, there are other types of software tools you may need to build your Yahoo! store.

Image Editor

If you are planning on taking digital pictures, scanning photos, or creating artwork of your product, an image-editing program is a must. An image-editing program will allow you to resize, crop, and touch up your photos. You might want to enhance your images because your customers are basing some of their purchasing decision on the quality and clarity of your product photos.

Some printers and scanners also come bundled with image-editing software. If you are planning on purchasing a printer or scanner, you may want to look into this before spending extra money on image-editing software. If your printer or scanner did not include image-editing software, here are some recommended image-editing programs.

The following recommended software can be downloaded via the company website and used on a trial basis free of charge for a limited time period. After the trial period, you can purchase a license and continue using the software.

- **Adobe Photoshop Elements**—Adobe Photoshop Elements (www.adobe.com) is the light version of Adobe Photoshop. Adobe introduced Elements for those who do not need all the tools of the full version of Photoshop and don't want to spend the extra money. Photoshop Elements is still a powerful photo-editing tool and will mostly likely satisfy all your editing needs. You can download Photoshop Elements for $89.99.

- **Macromedia Fireworks**—Fireworks (www.macromedia.com) is Macromedia's premier photo-editing program. If you're planning on using other Macromedia products, you might want to consider Fireworks for seamless integration between programs.

- **Corel Paint Shop Pro**—CorelDraw Paint Shop Pro (www.corel.com) is another great image-editing program. It starts at $69.00 and can be downloaded off Corel's website.

- **The Gimp**—GNU Image Manipulation Program (www.gimp.org) is a freely distributed software for photo retouching, image composition, and image authoring. Although not as popular as the other three, it's free!

The four programs mentioned above can be downloaded for a free trial. So pick a couple that work for you and try them out before you buy.

Web Browser

A web browser is a software application that lets users locate and display HTML web pages.

If you don't already have a web browser installed, you can download any of these browsers via the links below. Microsoft Internet Explorer is by far the most popular web browser, followed by Safari (Macintosh), then Firefox.

- **Internet Explorer**—Internet Explorer is Microsoft's own web browser, which comes bundled with all Microsoft operating systems. If you are running Microsoft Windows, you already have this browser installed on your computer.

- **Safari**—Safari is a Macintosh-specific web browser that's bundled with all new Macintosh computers. Safari can download web pages faster than other leading web browsers. Mac OS X is required for all Safari installations.

- **Firefox**—Firefox (firefox.com) made its debut in 2004 with more than 1 million downloads in the first four days. Firefox is continually gaining in popularity as an alternative to Microsoft's Internet Explorer, with advanced features such as an automatic pop-up blocker and live bookmarks that will allow you to view news headlines in the bookmark toolbar.

- **Netscape Navigator**—Once the predominant and main rival of Internet Explorer, Netscape Navigator (netscape.com) has lost market share, with less than 1% of users using the browser today.

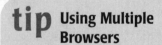

tip **Using Multiple Browsers**

It's also a great idea to download multiple browsers to test how your site looks and interacts in different browsers. This will guarantee that your customers have a similar web experience using their preferred web browser.

With Store Editor, you can use any standard web browser to create your store. Since it's all web-based, you can even access orders, site statistics, and customer data while you're away. This can be done on any computer with an Internet connection anywhere in the world.

Virus and Spyware Protection

The online world is filled with malicious software and spyware just waiting to infect your computer, track your every move online, and hijack your browser.

It's up to you to protect your computer from viruses, hackers, and privacy threats. Not only do you have to worry about a physical crash of your computer hardware, but a virus attack can cause a software crash, causing your computer system to be inoperable. Make sure you have antivirus and anti-spyware software installed and configured on your computer and sign up to get automatic updates. Antivirus and anti-spyware programs become useless unless you update them regularly.

So just what are viruses and spyware?

A virus is a manmade piece of code that can cause an unexpected event. Not only do you want to remove viruses from your computer, but you also want to block them before they cause damage to your computer. Having a virus protection software tool and getting frequent virus updates will help protect your computer. An example of antivirus software is Symantec's Norton Anti-Virus at www.symantec.com.

Web Resource

Latest Virus Threats

For a list of the latest virus threats and information, you can visit Symantec's website at http://securityresponse.symantec.com/avcenter/.

Ever wonder why you get those annoying pop-up ads even when you're not surfing the Web? You might have unintentionally downloaded a piece of spyware. Spyware is any piece of software that is unknowingly downloaded onto your computer that gathers information on your web surfing habits, and in some cases, collects personal information that you may have on your PC. Once installed, the spyware monitors user activity on the Internet and transmits that information in the background to someone else. Anti-spyware software helps protect your identity from being compromised, helps unwanted software from reporting your web activities, and prevents those unwanted Internet ads. Spyware can also send your personal information to malicious websites without your knowledge. Anti-spyware software will scan your computer and remove all unwanted spyware programs.

Here's a list of anti-spyware and virus protection software you should consider installing on your computer. Don't wait until your computer system becomes inoperable and you lose days, weeks, or months of business because of it.

- **Yahoo! Toolbar**—A free download that will block pop-up ads and protect your PC from spyware (toolbar.yahoo.com).
- **McAfee AntiSpyware and VirusScan**—Protect your computer, email, and attachments from known and unknown viruses (www.mcafee.com).

- **Norton AntiVirus and Internet Security AntiSpyware**—A competitor to McAfee's programs (www.symantec.com).
- **Lavasoft Ad-Aware**—A free copy of the Ad-Aware SE Personal Edition can be downloaded from the website (www.lavasoft.com).

Accounting Software

Show me the money! So how do you keep track of how many orders you have and how much money you are making? One of the things to look into is accounting software. Yahoo! Store Manger allows you to export order data in multiple formats that may be imported into your accounting software program, as seen in Figure 7.1. You can hire an accountant, but for the do-it-yourselfers, let's look at a few accounting software applications that can do the job for you.

- **QuickBooks by Intuit**—There is also an online edition of QuickBooks. Great for those who need to access their books while away (www.intuit.com).
- **Microsoft Money Small Business**—Similar to QuickBooks and integrates with MS Office (www.microsoft.com/money).
- **Peachtree by Sage**—A competitor to QuickBooks (www.peachtree.com).

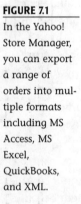

FIGURE 7.1

In the Yahoo! Store Manager, you can export a range of orders into multiple formats including MS Access, MS Excel, QuickBooks, and XML.

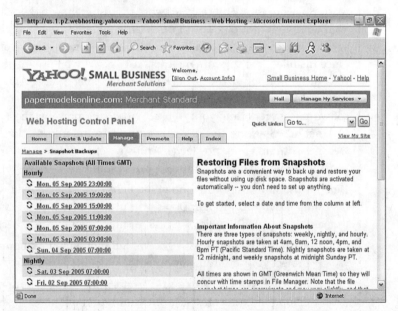

Setting Up the Home Office/Small Office

According to *Inc.* magazine, more small businesses were launched from the home than from a physical commercial site. One of the primary reasons, of course, is money. It takes far less capital to launch and maintain an eCommerce site than a physical storefront or office.

Still, there are things you need to consider when working a business from home.

Traffic and Liability—Though you will be selling products or services online, you must consider the kinds of traffic you will incur by bringing in inventory and shipping it out. Salespeople, mail and package carriers, and even clients for your service may have to visit your home for you to do business. Your neighbors may not appreciate the additional trucks and people that would continually parade through your neighborhood. You may need to check on the zoning regulations in your area to see what kind of business you can run from your home. In addition, your home may be part of a home owner's association and its CC&Rs (home owner's association rules and regulations) may prohibit any type of commercial activity from your home.

Then there's insurance. Will your insurance carrier cover accidents or other types of liability incidents that may occur on your site if they are business related? You may need business insurance.

Space Considerations—The available working area to do business is another consideration. First, where will you store your inventory if you're selling products? A home is not a warehouse. If your products are small and nonperishable, you can store them in your garage. But if you must carry a sizable number of large products, you will most probably need to rent storage space. Even if you can store your inventory in your home, if your business takes off, you will need more space for stock and for shipping and handling of the orders.

Second, consider your workspace itself. If you have your office in a room in your home, a computer, desk, printer, fax machine, copy machine, file cabinets, and so on will take up space, and as you grow your business, you will need more and more space. In a home that does double duty, either business or family, one or the other, will eventually be displaced. Think about privacy. Is your work space quiet? Can you close out noises from your home? Barking dogs and noisy children do not project a professional image.

Family Considerations—That brings us to your family life. Working at home is not all the pleasure it's cut out to be. Will your office be a private space of your home? What about family intrusions? Will you have separate home and business phone lines? If not, how will your family answer the phone for business? If you do have a separate business line, how do you keep the family from using your business phone? And how about the computer you use for business? Will other family members need it for their personal purposes? Then there's the possible resentment in your home from family members who feel you are not paying attention to them.

The key question here is "Can you keep your business and family life separate with a home business?" There are many distractions in a home that may keep you away from your business or slow your business down.

Basic Image Considerations

A business needs a professional image. A professional-looking Yahoo! store will accomplish this online. But there are other image criteria to consider.

Business Address—If you have a home-based business, you may or may not want to use your home address for business purposes. Deciding to use your address usually depends on what that address is. For example, suppose you live in an apartment. Your address of 1111 Park Lane might sound fine, but 1111 Park Lane, Apt. #4 may not project the image you are looking for. If you decide not to use your home address, you may opt for a P.O. box or use a mail service such as The UPS Store (www.theupsstore.com), and Mail Boxes Etc. (www.mbe.com). Using such a service will give you a private mailing address, access to delivery of large packages, and 24-hour access to your mailbox. Using a physical address will give your business a professional image. You can still decide to use a P.O. box, but customers tend to feel more comfortable doing business with you if there is a physical address. Another benefit of having a physical address is the ability to receive packages. Some companies will not deliver to a P.O. box.

Business Collateral Material—Take into account the look of your collateral material—business cards, letterhead, and envelopes. Spend some money and have a graphic designer create a professional-looking image for your company collateral material. Don't use those pre-perforated business cards you can buy at office stores. Nowadays, you can get 1,000 professionally printed business cards for less than $30. Also, your stationery, business cards, and promotional flyers are a great place to further promote your storefront. Make sure you add your URL and company email address to all your collateral material.

Business Phone—We spoke about a dedicated phone line for your business. Get one. And have it accessible only from your home office. Do the same with your fax line. Also, place a dedicated answering machine on your business line with a professional welcome message and your hours of operation for customer service calls. Customers like to know when they can personally reach you.

Finally, a good book for everything you should know about running a home business is *Start Your Own Home Business In No Time*. But if you decide that your home is not a suitable place to run your business then you might want to consider renting a small office.

Home Office Equipment Checklist

Besides the necessary computer and software needed to set up a Yahoo! store, here's a quick checklist of the equipment and services you will need to set up your home business.

- **Computer System and monitor**—Depending on your preference, a desktop or laptop computer will do just fine. If mobility is important to you and you are planning on working outside your office or on the road, you may want to consider purchasing a laptop.

- **Software**—Don't forget to set a budget aside for software. Depending on your needs, software can get expensive. Make sure you download and test trial versions before you buy. Most software will let you test drive the software for 30 days.

- **Fax, copier, scanner, and printer**—Most manufacturers offer an all-in-one fax, copier, scanner, and printer system. This is great if space is an issue. If you're planning on having a wireless network, you can purchase a network all-in-one system. A network system will allow you to use the device with your wireless computer anywhere in the house or office. Not only do you need a printer for documents and contracts, but printing invoices and packaging them with your customer orders will be part of your shipping process.

- **Furniture**—Planning on meeting clients at your office? Make sure you get quality furniture to make your office look professional. First impressions are everything. Let your clients know you're serious about your business.

- **Telephone**—If you're setting up a home office, having a second phone line will keep your personal calls separate from your business calls. You want to avoid having your family answer business calls. Many local phone companies offer a second line (marketing line) for a very low

($17) monthly fee.

- **Answering machine**—Since your store is not open for business 24/7, having an answering machine is a must. A customer in a different time zone across the globe could be trying to reach you during your non-business hours. Having an answering machine will ensure that you don't miss the call.

- **Fax/phone line switcher**—This is a small box that will answer your single line, detect whether it's a incoming fax or telephone call, and send it into either the phone or your fax machine (or your computer fax). It can be purchased for around $29.

- **File System**—You'll want to keep a well organized document filing system. This will ensure that you can retrieve documents or files quickly. Having a filing process in place early will also help you save time when taxes are due.

- **Internet Connection**—You can't have an online business without an Internet connection. If you are going to run a Yahoo! store, you will need to choose a broadband connection. The extra cost is worth the time savings. Time is money. Instead of spending countless hours staring at a slow-loading web page, you can market your website.

- **Digital Camera**—Planning on taking your own product photos? You can purchase a great digital camera for very little money. A minimum 3.2 Megapixel camera is recommended. You can purchase the camera online or at your local electronic store. Watch for specials in the Sunday paper.

Now that you've set up your home office, you're ready to consider your Yahoo! store. In the next chapter, we will help you choose the right Yahoo! store merchant package that fits your business needs.

**What You'll Learn
in This Chapter**

• Important consider-
ations in choosing a
solutions package

• Compare different
solutions with a
convenient table

• Advantages and
disadvantages of
using a Yahoo!
store

Choosing a Merchant
Solutions Package

So you have your unique selling position designed,
your business plan competed, and the tools and location to build and operate your home or small business.
Now it's time to see what Yahoo! store can offer you to
build your online storefront. That is, it's time to choose
a Yahoo! store Merchant Solution Package.

Yahoo! Merchant Solutions is Yahoo!'s turnkey
eCommerce solution for building, managing, and marketing your online store. Merchant Solutions includes
domain name; business email; web hosting with secure
shopping cart and online credit card processing; sales
reports and site statistics; advance catalog and inventory management; and the option to participate in
Yahoo! Shopping. Depending upon your initial needs,
Yahoo! Merchant Solutions offers three packages to
choose from: Starter, Standard, and Professional. You
would choose one these Merchant Solutions to start.
But as your business grows, you can easily upgrade
your Yahoo! storefront and take advantage of the
many valuable options that the Yahoo! store Merchant
Solutions offer. Let's take a look at each merchant
package and compare them to one another so you can
choose the package that fits your business best.

Yahoo Merchant Solutions

So which package is right for you? Choosing a merchant solution package will depend on your business process needs, cost of web hosting, and the features you would like to utilize. The Yahoo! Merchant Solutions packages offer a number of features that will make your online storefront and its management easy and efficient, and include the flowing features:

- **Order Processing**—Yahoo! Merchant Solutions comes with a suite of tools to help you with order processing, such as a central management system that will allow you to view, approve, or deny orders; accept multiple forms of payment; receive orders via email or fax; send status updates; automatically calculate taxes during the checkout process; and customize risk tools to prevent fraud.

- **Shipping Tools**—Yahoo! Merchant Solutions gives you the ability to set up multiple shipping options such as express, priority, ground, and/or air. Merchant Solutions also is integrated with UPS to generate tracking and shipping labels.

- **Product Category and Inventory Management**—Catalog Manager allows you to view, sort, edit, and organize your product information. You can also receive alerts when your product availability falls under a predetermined level.

- **Merchandising**—Marketing tools such as gift certificates, a coupon manager, and a cross-selling engine are some of the options that comes with the Merchant Solutions Standard and Professional packages.

- **Statistics**—Keep track of what's hot and what's not. Generate easy-to-read reports to see how well your products are selling. Track visitor rates to see how your marketing campaigns are doing or view what keywords customers used to find your website on major search engines.

- **Exclusive Discounts and Marketing Services**—As a merchant, you have access to discounts to list your product on popular shopping websites such as Yahoo! Shopping, www.shopping.com, and www.bizrate.com. Also available are third-party tools to help promote your business such as email marketing solutions, affiliate programs, and search engine submission.

- **Personalized Domain Name**—As a Merchant Solutions customer, you can register your own domain name (www.yourdomain.com) free of charge as long as your account is active.

- **Customer Support**—Help is just a phone call away. Customer support is available toll-free 24 hours, 7 days a week.

- **Website Management**—Included in your package is 10 Gigabytes of data storage. Additional disk space is also available at an additional charge.

- **Website Design**—Store Editor comes with easy-to-use templates to build your store. Merchant Solutions also supports other HTML building tools such as Dreamweaver, Frontpage, and Yahoo! SiteBuilder.

- **Email**—Up to 100 email accounts are included with every package. Get up to 2GB of storage per email account. Merchant Solutions supports POP and SMTP access so you can use popular email software tools such as Microsoft Outlook. Tired of getting email spam? SpamGuard Plus junk email protection helps prevent those unwanted emails.

- **Site Security**—Every customer order is protected with SSL security for all transactions, order processing, and shopping cart pages to prevent fraud. Merchant Solutions also has a built-in backup system just in case you need to restore your files.

Table 8.1 compares all three merchant solution packages; their prices range from $39.95 to $299.95 per month.

Table 8.1   ComparisonChart

Package	Starter	Standard	Professional
Monthly Hosting fee	$39.95	$99.95	$299.95
One-time setup fee	$50	$50	$50
Transaction fee	1.5%	1%	0.75%
Best plan for merchants expecting sales of	$0–$11,999/mo.	$12,000–$79,999/mo.	More than $80,000/mo.
Ordering Processing			
Accept credit card payments online (PayPal account or merchant account required*)	✓	✓	✓
Configurable Risk Tools to verify	✓	✓	✓
Shopping cart and secure checkout process	✓	✓	✓
Set up tax tables for automatic calculation in checkout	✓	✓	✓
Central order management system (view, approve, and print orders)	✓	✓	✓

Table 8.1 ComparisonChart (continued)

Package	Starter	Standard	Professional
Automated order confirmations and status update emails	✓	✓	✓
Receive orders via fax or email	Email only	✓	✓
Post order data in real-time to external or applications		✓	✓
Shipping Tools			
Set up shipping methods and rate calculation rules	✓	✓	✓
Automated UPS shipment processing, tracking, and shipping label generation	✓	✓	✓
Export orders to UPS Worldship			✓
Product Catalog and Inventory Management			
Catalog Manager (view, sort, edit, and organize product information)	✓	✓	✓
Upload and download product information into Catalog Manager so it can be managed offline	✓	✓	✓
Track inventory by option (color, size, and so on)	✓	✓	✓
Receive inventory alerts if quantity drops below predetermined levels	✓	✓	✓
Merchandising			
Gift certificates		✓	✓
Cross-sell engine		✓	✓
Coupon Manager		✓	✓
Trackable links for affiliate and other revenue sharing programs	✓	✓	
Statistics			
Configurable sales reports and graphs (items sold, orders, revenue, and so on)	✓	✓	✓
Page view and referring site statistics	✓	✓	✓
Repeat orders by customers	✓	✓	✓
Click trails (shows pathways customers take through your site when they purchase)		✓	✓
Frequent search topics for your site		✓	✓
Exclusive Discounts on Marketing Services			
Listings in shopping destinations (Yahoo! Shopping, Shopping.com, BizRate)	✓	✓	✓
Search engine keyword ads (Yahoo! Sponsored optimization (Search, Google AdWords)	✓	✓	✓

Table 8.1   ComparisonChart (continued)

Package	Starter	Standard	Professional
Search engine submissions and Submitnet)	✓	✓	✓
Ad performance tracking (KeyWordMax)	✓	✓	✓
Email marketing solution (Got)	✓	✓	✓
Direct marketing lists (infoUSA)	✓	✓	✓
Affiliate programs (Commission Junction)	✓	✓	✓
Personalized Domain Name			
Domain name registration	✓	✓	✓
Domain locking to help prevent unauthorized transfers	✓	✓	✓
Yahoo! Private Domain Registration to help protect your privacy**	+ $0.75/mo.	+ $0.75/mo.	+ $0.75/mo.
Website sub-domains	500	500	500
Customer Support			
24-hour toll-free phone support	✓	✓	✓
Priority email and online help	✓	✓	✓
Website Management			
Disk space for storing files	10 GB	10 GB	10 GB
Data transfer (bandwidth)/month	200 GB	200 GB	200 GB
Multi-user FTP for putting files on server	✓	✓	✓
Website Design			
Easy-to-use wizard and templates to build a store fast	✓	✓	✓
Yahoo! SiteBuilder software (includes 380+ customizable website templates and robust tools)	✓	✓	✓
Yahoo! Merchant Solutions Extension for Dreamweaver	✓	✓	✓
Support for Microsoft FrontPage***	✓	✓	✓
Perl, PHP, and MySQL for building interactive sites****	✓	✓	✓
Email			
Yahoo! Business Mail accounts	100	100	100
Email storage (per account)	2GB	2GB	2GB
POP and SMTP email access	✓	✓	✓
SpamGuard Plus junk email protection	✓	✓	✓
Norton AntiVirus screening and cleaning	✓	✓	✓

Table 8.1   ComparisonChart (continued)

Package	Starter	Standard	Professional
Site Security			
Password-protected user accounts	100	100	100
Regular website backups and restores	✓	✓	✓
SSL security for all transactions, order processing, and shopping cart pages	✓	✓	✓
Assign access privileges to Store Manager tools	✓	✓	✓

* PayPal and merchant account are not included with the Merchant Solutions account.

** Private domain registration is available for an additional $.07 per month.

*** Microsoft FrontPage is a third-party software tool that must be purchased separately.

**** Does not work with the Product Catalog and Store Tags.

As you can see from the chart, Yahoo! Merchant Solutions has plenty of features to build, manage, and market your site.

For new features and an updated comparison chart, please visit http://smallbusiness.yahoo.com/merchant/compare.php.

As we mentioned previously, you can easily upgrade your merchant solution package as your business grows. If you are just starting out and don't want to spend the extra money, you can sign-up for the Starter package and upgrade later. Once you're ready to take full advantage of all the other features the Standard and Professional packages have to offer, just log in to your store manager, click on the Change or Cancel Plan link, and then click on the Upgrade link under the Merchant Solutions package you would like to upgrade to (see Figure 8.1). Yahoo! Merchant Solutions will automatically adjust your monthly invoice.

tip The merchandising marketing features such as cross-sell engine, coupon manager, and gift certificates that are included with the Standard package make it worthwhile to spend the extra money. With those marketing features, you can up sell and create repeat customers.

Building Your Store—Store Editor Versus Web Hosting

Okay. You chose a merchant package that meets your business needs. Now you have to build your online store. Yahoo! Merchant Solutions has two different tools for hosting and building your online store. They are Store Editor and Web Hosting. Which options you should choose will depend on your needs and technical capabilities. Table 8.2 will show important differences between each tool.

FIGURE 8.1

Setup fees are waived when you upgrade to a more powerful Merchant Solutions package.

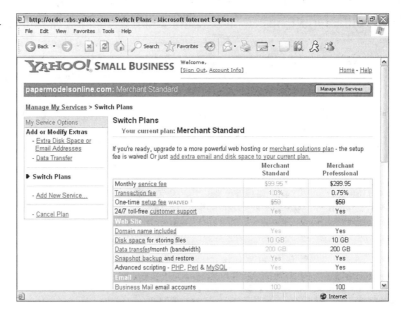

Table 8.2   Differences Between Store Editor and Web Hosting

	Store Editor	Web Hosting
Creating new web pages	You create your web pages in the Store Editor using any standard web browser.	You create your web pages using an HTML software tool such as MacromediaDreamweaver.*
Publishing your website	Just click the Publish button on the toolbar in Store Editor.	Upload your web pages via an FTP client or Yahoo! File Manager to your hosting account.
URL (Uniform Resource Locator) or web address of your website	Your web pages are published to the sub-domain "store"; for example, store. yourdomain.com.	Your web pages are published to the "www." sub-domain; for example, www.yourdomain.com.
Ease of development	If you are new to building a web page, do not know HTML, and want to create a store as quickly as possible, the Store Editor may be the right choice. To create products, all you need to do is fill out the forms and upload your images by using a browser. The Store Editor will create the product pages for you.	If you know HTML and want to use a program such as Dreamweaver and want to customize your store, building your store in Web Hosting may be right for you. Using Web Hosting will require you to import the Catalog Manager data or manually insert Store Tags and Store Modules.

Table 8.2   Differences Between Store Editor and Web Hosting (continued)

	Store Editor	Web Hosting
Ease of design customization	It is less easy to customize your store layout and look using Store Editor. Although there are many options to customize your layout using variables, you may find it difficult to customize the store to your exact specifications.	If you are experienced with HTML and want to have more control over the layout and look of the store, this might be the right choice for you. If you are familiar with using tools such as Dreamweaver, this may be more intuitive. Web Hosting also allows you to use features such as PHP/MySQL and Perl.
Your HTML building software tool experience	If you don't have experience coding HTML or any HTML building software, using Store Editor with get your site up and running in a short amount of time using just your web browser. Store Editor comes with a preset look along with navigation buttons on the left side.	If you are experience and comfortable using HTML building software, you may prefer using Web Hosting. Web Hosting may take more work but will give you the flexibility of customization to your store.

* For more information on Dreamweaver go to www.macromedia.com.

Deciding How to Build Your Store

When deciding between the Store Editor tool and Web Hosting, there are three key issues that will affect your decision:

- How quickly do you want to get your site up and running for business?

- How much do you want to customize your site?

- How much experience do you have using HTML building software?

In this book, we will focus on users with no or very little HTML experience who want to use the Store Editor to build their stores as quickly as possible. If you are familiar with using HTML building software and want to use Web Hosting instead of Store Editor, please refer to our second book *Making a Living with Your Yahoo! Store*.

caution Switching from Store Editor to Web Hosting can be a challenge and very time consuming. You may find yourself recreating all of your product pages. There are no easy conversion tools to help you export your Store Editor web pages and images into Web Hosting. You may even want to contact other Yahoo! store owners to see why they choose one over the other.

If Yahoo!'s Store Editor will build a storefront for you, why consider the Web Hosting option?

Web Hosting gives you more control over the look and feel of your store. It's great if you are familiar with HTML or HTML building software such as Dreamweaver or Microsoft's FrontPage. It will take more time to build your store than with Store Editor, but Web Hosting will allow you to use features such as PHP, ASP, Perl, and MySQL.

PHP and *ASP* are scripting languages that can be embedded inside your HTML and allow web pages to be dynamically generated from a database. *Perl* is also a programming language that is used to perform database access, networking, and more. *MySQL* is an open source database that can be used to store and retrieve data. Using MySQL in combination with Perl and/or PHP/ASP, you can create dynamic web pages such as product search pages, interactive forms, and dynamic postings of product reviews.

Most businesses prefer to use the Web Hosting option because they can customize the store to their clients' specific needs using popular HTML building tools.

Using HTML Building Software Tools

If you do decide to go the Web Hosting route then you should have experience with Dreamweaver, SiteBuilder, or some other HTML building tool. Let's take a look at a few of them.

Dreamweaver is Macromedia's premier WYSIWYG (What You See Is What You Get) HTML authoring tool (www.macromedia.com). Dreamweaver is a popular software program that is widely used by professional web designers and developers. Yahoo! Merchant Solutions extensions for Dreamweaver are also available. Once you download and install the extensions from the Merchant Solutions website, you can use commands in the Yahoo! menu of Dreamweaver to quickly manage and update your product catalog with product page wizard. You can easily insert product information with a few mouse clicks.

You can download a trial version of Macromedia Dreamweaver at macromedia.com/software/dreamweaver/.

Yahoo! SiteBuilder is Yahoo!'s free HTML authoring tool. SiteBuilder comes with more than 380 templates to choose from. SiteBuilder is available for stores with 100 or fewer products.

For more information and to download SiteBuilder, please visit help.yahoo.com/help/us/store/edit/sitebuilder.

FIGURE 8.2
Macromedia Dreamweaver is the most popular HTML building tool among web designers and developers.

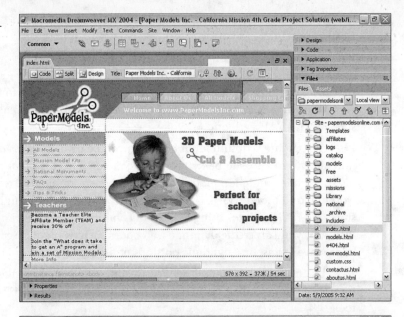

FIGURE 8.3
SiteBuilder also comes with a Store Product Wizard where you can upload all your product data to easily create product pages.

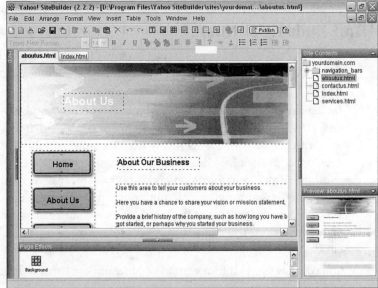

Store Editor is an online tool that lets you develop and host your online store using just a web browser on any computer with an Internet connection. It's easy as point, click, and fill in the blanks—perfect for those who want to get their site up and running as quickly as possible.

It also comes with a generic template that you can customize. Using variables, you can customize attributes such as text font, buttons, backgrounds, link color, image dimensions, and more.

Yahoo Talk   *Variables* are design elements that affect the look of every page in the store.

Store Editor will allow you to create or update your store in an online staging area, and once you're ready to go live, all you have to do is click on the Publish button.

All the pages are hosted on the "store" sub-domain for your account. For example, if your web site address is www.yourdomain.com, the store website address would be store.yourdomain.com. Yahoo! also allows you to direct the homepage of your website to the store.yourdomain.com sub-domain. For more information, visit help.yahoo.com/help/us/store/manage/sitesettings/sitesettings-27.html.

FIGURE 8.4

A typical Yahoo! store template.

Customization with Store Editor

Store Editor comes with a standard template. You can add a background image; change background color, link color, button size, font size, and font type; change image dimensions; upload your logo; change your navigation button properties; add custom variables; and much more. Store Editor comes with an easy-to-use form to change any of the variable options.

FIGURE 8.5

Homepage of
the Store Editor.

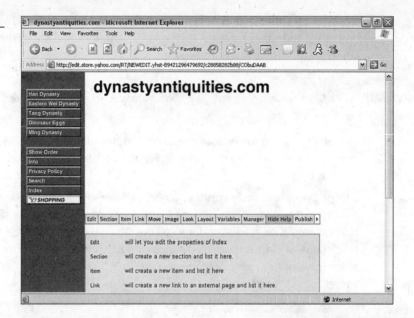

Yahoo! store comes with a standard template look and feel. Although you can change simple variables such as background color, button size, button color, and font type, you will not be able to create a unique look and feel unless you modify the template using RTML. The Yahoo! store standard template was designed for those who do not need a unique custom design and want to quickly get their stores up and running. In

> **caution** Yahoo! Merchant Solutions customer service cannot offer phone or email support on RTML and templates. Merchant Solutions customers will need to find outside consultants for assistance.

order to create a new template with your own unique design, you will need to learn RTML or hire an RTML designer.

RTML is Yahoo!'s proprietary language for building store templates. RTML is for advanced programmers who don't want to use the Store Editor standard templates and want to customize their store's design templates. If you would like to customize your store, you may want to look into Web Hosting before attempting to learn RTML. You may find it easier to use WYSIWYG authoring tools such as Dreamweaver to customize your store layout.

You can also visit Yahoo!'s Designer Directory to find RTML programmers at smallbusiness.yahoo.com/merchant/designdir.php.

RTML Resources

Here are some resources to help with your RTML development.

- RTML Quick-start guide to modifying templates (www.monitus.com/ebook.htm)
- Unofficial Guide to Yahoo! Store Templates (www.ytimes.info/bookabyahsto.html)
- Yahoo!'s Designer Directory (smallbusiness.yahoo.com/merchant/designdir.php)

Clicks Versus Bricks

With Merchant Solutions, you have the ability to sell hard goods (physical products you need to ship) or soft goods (downloadable products such as software, photos (JPGs), PDFs, or ebooks). If you are planning on selling a combination of hard goods and soft goods or only soft goods, you may want to be aware of a few potential issues.

Since fulfillment of soft goods happen immediately, store owners may not be able to prevent fraud orders. For downloadable products, a link to the product is presented immediately on the confirmation page at the end of the customer order process. This is unlike hard goods, where store owners are notified of the order and any flagged invalid credit card data before the fulfillment takes place. Therefore, the customer will already obtain your downloadable product before you can verify and process the order. With Merchant Solutions, the only information the customer needs to process the order is a valid credit card number. If the credit card address, expiration date, name on the credit card, or three-digit verification number on the back of the card are invalid, the order is still processed but will be flagged for further verification by the merchant. You can set up the system to automatically charge the credit card, but that still will not match the credit card number with the other customer information. If it's a true fraudulent order, you could be charging the credit card of someone who did not place the order. If you see a pattern of fraud orders, you can use the Risk Tools to block a certain IP address or a range of IP addresses from placing an order at your store. This doesn't prevent the person from going to the next coffee shop and doing the same thing, but it will sure slow them down.

Another issue that will arise if you are thinking of selling a combination of hard goods and soft goods is the confusion of shipping options. In the Shipping Manager, you can set up multiple shipping options such as express, priority, downloadable, ground, and/or air. But what happens if a customer orders a soft good and a hard good in the same order? Or if they only order a soft good? The Shipping Manager isn't smart enough to not display the other shipping options when someone orders a soft good. This can cause confusion when a customer is presented with all those options during the checkout process. They might even select the wrong shipping option and accidentally be charged extra for shipping when there is nothing to be shipped. A workaround to this issue is to manually notify the customer during the checkout process. You can add a warning message on the checkout page so the customer is aware of the shipping options, which will most likely not be read. This workaround will not dummy-proof the ordering process but will somewhat reduce phone calls and tech support.

Advantages and Disadvantages of Using Yahoo! Store

Like anything in business, there are both advantages and disadvantages to choices you make. The trick is to choose a solution that is more advantage than disadvantage. Yahoo! Merchant Solutions are no different. So let's look at the advantages and disadvantages that they offer.

Advantages

The list below outlines some of the advantages of using the Yahoo! store. Yahoo! Merchant Solutions is a complete eCommerce solution that will help you build, manage, and market your store.

- Turnkey solution—Everything you need to get your site up and running.
- Easy-to-use interface—Page wizards and tools to help you create your products.
- Efficiency—Gets your site up and running quickly.
- 24/7 toll-free customer support—Need help? Customer service representatives are standing by to answer your questions.
- Email—Get 100 email accounts with 2GB of storage per account
- Secure credit card processing—Give your customer peace of mind with SSL (Secure Socket Layer) when transferring sensitive data over the Internet.
- Low monthly fees—Low-risk monthly fee to get you started selling worldwide.

- Web statistics—View website visitor trends and generate sales reports.

- Backup system—Complete built-in recovery system.

- Ability to accept multiple payment options—Ability to accept a variety of credits cards on your website.

- Shipping tools—Built-in shipping tools to help you streamline your shipping process. Ability to notify your customers when their orders are being shipped.

- Marketing tools and discounts—By being a Yahoo! Merchant Solutions customer, you have the ability to utilize Yahoo!'s marketing tools to increase your sales and discounts to popular marketing services.

- Continuous development and new features—With a strong business partner such as Yahoo!, you can guarantee that Yahoo! will continually improve and develop new store features.

- The power and name recognition of Yahoo!—With a trusted name such as Yahoo!, customers will feel safe and secure when doing business with you.

Disadvantages

Beware of some of the limitations when using the Yahoo! store. Having knowledge of some of the disadvantages will help you develop workarounds when building and managing your store. The following is a list of some of the disadvantages of using the Yahoo! store.

- Dedicated customer support—Although Yahoo! has 24/7 customer support, you don't get the same customer representative every time you call in. You may find yourself repeating the issue over and over again.

- Risk Tools—Yahoo! comes with a suite of tools to help identify and prevent fraud orders. When a customer places an order with a credit card, the credit card is immediately verified to make sure it's a valid credit card. The AVS (Address Verification System) and CVV (Card Verification Value) check the system to make sure that the information matches. Although the AVS and CVV information is verified, the system will flag orders, but not deny fraudulent orders. It's up to the storeowner to either accept the order if it's flagged or deny the order based on further investigations. The only valid information that the system needs to process the order is a valid credit card number. The system will process the order even with an incorrect address, name, city, ZIP Code, expiration date, and card verification number. The extra work involved to make sure that the credit card belongs to the customer can slow down the shipping process. Merchant Solutions does come with tools such as IP blocking if you see a pattern of fraud or suspicious orders from the same range of IP addresses.

In Chapter 14, "To Do List—Managing Workflow," we will look at how to review orders for fraud and identify the warning signs.

- Downloadable products—Planning on selling downloadable software, photos, PDFs, or ebooks? Since fulfillment of downloadable goods happens immediately, store owners may not be able to prevent fraud. For downloadable products, a link to the product is presented immediately on the confirmation page. This is unlike hard products, where store owners are notified of the order and any flagged credit card data before the fulfillment takes place for further investigation.

- Nonintegrated affiliate program—Planning on using an affiliate program to generate more sales? Even though you can use third-party affiliate programs or Yahoo!'s recommended affiliate software program, Commission Junction, you might find it tedious to track down a refund/credit order generated by one of your affiliates. Since the two ordering systems are not integrated, when you give someone credit in your Yahoo! store system, it does not automatically send that credit to the affiliate software system.

- Customization with Store Editor—In order to customize the Store Editor templates, you will need to learn RTML or hire an RTML consultant.

Now that you are familiar with all the options you have for building your online store with Yahoo! Merchant Solutions, go to http://smallbusiness.yahoo.com/merchant/ and sign up for an account (see Figure 8.6). The next chapter will focus on those who do not know HTML and want to get their sites up and running as quickly as possible. You'll learn how to build your store with Store Editor, customize your site, and publish your site for business. So let's get started!

FIGURE 8.6

Yahoo!
Merchant
Solutions pro-
vide an easy-to-
use sign up
form and
domain name
search.

Creating Your Yahoo! Store

Now that you have chosen your Yahoo! Merchant Solutions package and signed up for an account, let's get started building your store.

In this chapter, will focus on those who don't know or have very little experience with HTML (a web page markup language) and want to use Store Editor's easy to use online forms to build their storefront as quickly as possible. As an example, we'll actually build a real live Chinese Antiquities online store (store.dynastyantiquities.com) and publish it for business. This site will sell antiques from the Chinese dynasties. You'll learn how to add products, images, and sections, customize your page layout, and publish the site.

Planning Your Website Content

Plan your website content before you start creating your website. When planning your website, keep the goal of your site in mind. Consider how your target audience will navigate through your site and not how you would navigate through your site. Take a look at competitors or other successful online retailers to learn how they structured their websites.

Although each website is unique, there are certain essential elements that make up a winning website:

- **Persuasive home page**: Your home page should include your logo, top-level category navigation menu, unique selling position, featured products, special offers, and new items.

- **Navigation menu**: How will your customers move from one page to another? They will need to know where they are at all times. Keep your top-level navigation menu consistent throughout all your pages.

- **Section pages**: Group related products. Creating categories help organize your products, especially if you have a large number of items.

- **Item pages**: Your item pages need to provide vital detailed information about the product. Provide a clear picture of your product. Add multiple views of the product if necessary.

- **Contact us/about us page**: Provide an overview of your company, company address and phone number, return policy, technical support email or phone number, and shipping information. Many customers will want to make sure that you are a real live company.

- **Privacy policy**: A privacy policy will ensure customers that their personal information will not be misused.

- **Shopping cart/checkout page**: Make sure your customers can easily access the shopping cart or checkout page to proceed to finalizing their transactions. These pages are created automatically based on a form you complete.

Consider creating a flowchart when drafting your website content. Get different perspectives from others by showing them your proposed site layout. Others may pick up something that you might have missed.

Organizing Your Materials

Before you begin creating your first product, gather all the information and files you need to build your store. This will help you keep organized and get your store up and running as quickly as possible. Consider using a spreadsheet program such as Microsoft Excel to help organize your product data. You can use Excel to cut and paste your product information into the Product Add form to eliminate having to type most of your data again. If someone else is helping you add product descriptions or pricing, you can print out the Excel spreadsheet and have the person fill in the blanks or you can just email them the Excel file. This will help you save time and speed up the process.

Required Fields

The Add Item form contains 23 product properties also known as *fields*. You can enter data, select data from drop-down menus, or upload images. Each product must contain the following required fields:

tip The ID is also used for uploading multiple images. If you name the image file to match its corresponding product ID, the system automatically places the image in the respective product page. For example, if you have a product with an ID of zd100, the image filename must be zd100.jpg.

- **ID**: A unique ID for internal use only. IDs are not displayed to the customer and must not contain any symbols, spaces, or non-alphanumeric characters. Make sure you come up with a naming convention and stick with it.
- **Name**: The name of your product. The name will also be used as the title tag for the product's web page.
- **Code**: A unique code. You can use a product SKU (Stock Keeping Unit) if available.
- **Price**: The amount you want to sell the item for.
- **Orderable**: Is the product orderable? If marked no, the buy button will not display.
- **Taxable**: Whether the product should be taxed. If marked no, no taxes will be added.

Optional Fields

The following fields are also part of the Add Item form. These fields were designed to accommodate a wide range of products. Depending on your product, you might or might not choose to enter product data into these fields.

- **Sale-price**: The new discounted amount.
- **Ship-weight**: The amount the product weighs. Can be used to calculate shipping cost.

- **Image**: Product photograph you can upload.

- **Options**: Product options such as size and color.

- **Headline**: Any text in the Headline field will replace the page name. A more descriptive name can be added here for display.

- **Caption**: The text for the description of the product. The text will be displayed underneath the Headline.

- **Abstract**: Used when text is needed for a description on another page.

- **Download**: If you are selling soft goods (downloadable products), you can upload the files here.

- **Product-URL**: The exact web page location of the product page. This will help customers go back to the product page during checkout. The product title will be linked to the URL you enter. If you are using Store Editor or Catalog Manager, this will automatically be generated for you even though a URL will not be displayed in the field.

These are the default fields in the Add Item form. You can also add your own custom fields by editing the product tables in Catalog Manager. Don't feel as if you have to add data to every optional field. The fields are there to accommodate a wide range of products.

FIGURE 9.1

Add Item form using Store Editor.

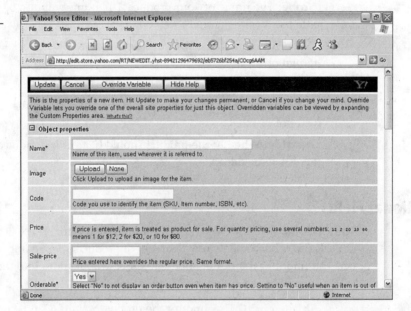

Product Images

What's a product description without a picture? So, gather all the product photos you want to use. Consider putting them all in one file folder on your computer for easy access. If you need to adjust color, resize, or brighten an image, make sure you do that before uploading your images. You can always go back and upload the images again or change an image later, but it's easier to do it the first time around since you're already in the Add Item form.

tip Product descriptions— Spend some time and write a description that will help sell your product. Research other websites to see what the buzz words are to entice the customer. Survey potential customers to see what they are looking for and make sure you include that information.

Getting Started

If you haven't already done so, go ahead and log in to your Merchant Solutions account at smallbusiness.yahoo.com/ merchant/.

Once you log in, it will take you to the Manage My Services home page. From here, you can go to the Store Manager to work on your store; the Web Hosting Control Panel to view stats, manage files, and view recent backups; the Domain Control Panel to manage advance DNS settings and sub-domains; and the Email Control Panel to manage and create email accounts.

caution If you are planning on using the product description or product photo from the manufacturer, make sure you get permission in writing first. You do not want to infringe on any copyright. Also for better search engine placement, consider rewording the product description that came from the manufacturer. This will reduce your chances of getting penalized by the search engine's duplicate content filter. Make sure your page contains at least 80% original content.

The flowchart shown in Figure 9.2 has been provided to show you how to navigate to the different control panels and to the Store Editor and Catalog Manager.

Getting to Know the Store Manager

Go ahead and click on the Store Manager link so we can take a look at all the tools and options to help build your store. Make sure you click through each service to familiarize yourself with what Yahoo! Merchant Solutions has to offer.

FIGURE 9.2

Control panel flowchart.

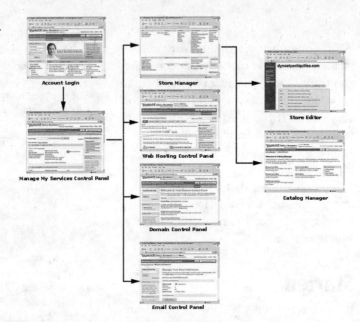

From the Store Manager, you can process your orders, edit your store, customize your order form, set up shipping rates, set up tax tables, view statistics, add users to the account, promote the site, and much more. As you can see in Figure 9.3, there are a lot of tools and properties to help build and customize your store.

FIGURE 9.3

Store Manager.

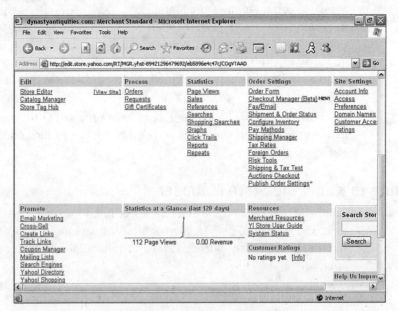

Creating Your First Section

If you have a lot of products that need to be categorized and grouped, you will want to create sections for easy navigation. You do not want to have hundreds of products on one page. Once you create a section, a button will be created in the navigation menu. In this example, we have various antiques from the Chinese dynasties. We want to group them by their particular dynasty. The first Chinese dynasty is the Zhou Dynasty. Let's create our first section.

1. In the Store Editor, click on the Section button on the toolbar.

2. When the form appears, the following properties are available. The only property that is required is the Name field, but we'll go ahead and add information in the Headline and Caption fields, as seen in Figure 9.4.

   a. Name

   b. Image

   c. Headline

   d. Caption

   e. Abstract

   f. Icon

   g. Inset

   h. Label

   i. Product URL

   j. Path

3. Once you finish filling out the form, go ahead and click Update. Once you click Update, your new section will appear. As you can see in Figure 9.5, the Zhou Dynasty button has been created under the Home button.

To create additional sections, click on the Up button to go back to the home page and repeat the previous steps. You can create as many sections as you wish. If you forget to click on the Up button, a subsection will be created within the newly created Zhou Dynasty section and a button will not be created in the navigation menu.

Now that we have created a section, let's take a look at adding our first product.

FIGURE 9.4
Add Section
form.

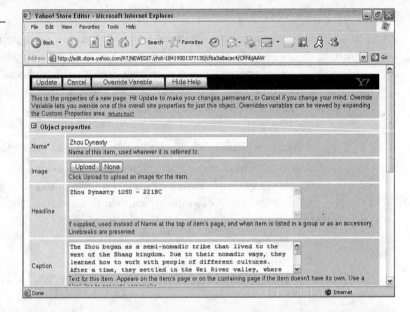

FIGURE 9.4
Add Section
form.

FIGURE 9.5
The Zhou
Dynasty button
was created as a
result of creat-
ing a section, as
described in the
demo.

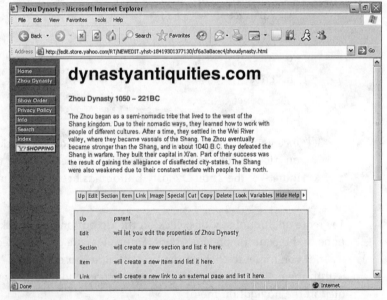

Two Ways to Add a Product

There are two ways to add products to your online store. You can use the Store
Editor or the Catalog Manager. Every time you create a product in Catalog
Manager, the product is also created in Store Editor. And vice versa, if you are

using Store Editor to create a product, a product record is also created in the Catalog Manager. So whatever method you choose, the product data will be available in both Store Editor and Catalog Manager. Although you can create products in both, we recommend creating the product in Store Editor and using the Store Manager to manage your products. We'll show you how to create your product using both methods. In the following example, we'll create a product in the Zhou Dynasty section we created earlier.

caution If you add a product before adding a section in Store Editor, a button will also be created with the product name in the menu column. This is fine if you have a few products and want them displayed in your navigation menu. If you have a lot of products and want to categorize them, you will want to create a section first before you create the product. If you make a mistake and create the product first, you can always move the product into its section later.

Store Editor

Using Store Editor will help you visually place the products where you want them to go. All you have to do is navigate to the particular section and add the item.

Before we get started, let's get to know the Editor Toolbar in Store Editor. To get to the toolbar, click on the Store Editor link in the Store Manager. The toolbar will appear on every page in Store Editor as shown in Figure 9.6.

FIGURE 9.6

Screenshot Editor toolbar.

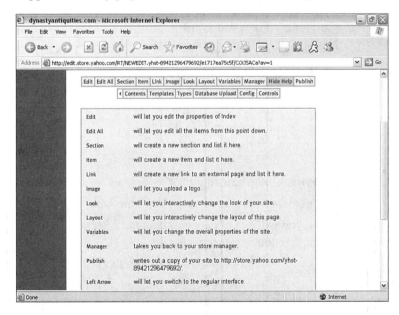

Standard Edit Toolbar

- **Edit**: Edit the properties of the page or product you are on.
- **Edit All**: Allows you to edit all the products from this point down.
- **Section**: Create a section and a button will be created in the navigation menu.
- **Item**: Create a new item.
- **Link**: Create a hyperlink to an external or internal page.
- **Image**: Lets you upload an image.
- **Look**: Change the look of the site.
- **Layout**: Change the layout of the page.
- **Variables**: Change the overall properties of the site.
- **Manager**: Takes you back to the Store Manager page.
- **Publish**: Upload the development store to your live store.

Advanced Editor Toolbar

The advanced toolbar will appear as a second row underneath the standard toolbar when you click on the red triangle next to the Publish button.

- **Contents**: Takes you to the table of contents or tree of the site.
- **Template**: View all built-in and custom templates.
- **Types**: Takes you to the built-in and custom types page.
- **Database Upload**: Lets you upload data files to the store.
- **Config**: Lets you edit properties such as editor toolbar location, default templates, and default items in Store Editor.
- **Controls**: Set Store Editor properties such as mode and editor entry page, or access advanced features such as search, multiple image upload, and edit multiple items.

Creating Your First Product with Store Editor

1. In Store Manager, click on the Store Editor Link as shown in Figure 9.7.
2. If you want to place the product in a section, navigate to that particular section.
3. On the Editor toolbar, click on the Item button.
4. Input the information for you product on the Add Item form as shown in Figure 9.8. You do not have to enter data into every field. As

mentioned earlier in the chapter, the only required fields are ID, Name, Code, Taxable, Orderable, and Price. In Store Editor, the ID is automatically generated for you.

5. To upload a product image, click on the Upload button next to the Image property. Another page will appear with a dialog box so you can browse and upload your image. Once you are done, click on the Send button. This will take you back to the Add Item form.

6. Once you are done, click on the Update button at the top of the form.

Great! Now you have created your first product. To create additional products, just repeat the previous steps, starting with step 2.

To view a video on how to create a product with Store Editor, go to www.MyEcommerceSuccess.com.

FIGURE 9.7
Store Editor link in Store Manager.

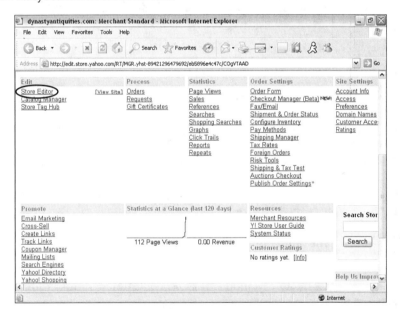

Catalog Manager

Let's take a look at a few advantages of using Catalog Manager.

- **Viewing and sorting products**: You can view up to 100 products at a time. You can also sort your products by any of the fields. Want to sort by all your products by price? All you have to do is click on the price link.

- **Organizing your products by tables**: You can categorize your products by creating separate tables. Tables are perfect for seasonal products. You can create or upload a Christmas product line table and delete the whole table once the season is over.

- **Deleting or moving multiple items**: It's easy to delete or move multiple items with the item page.

- **Downloading product data**: Catalog Manager has an upload and download tool. You can download a CSV data file of all your products. In Catalog Manager, you can use the Add Item page to add a product, or add another product in the CSV data file and upload the file.

FIGURE 9.8

Add Item form.

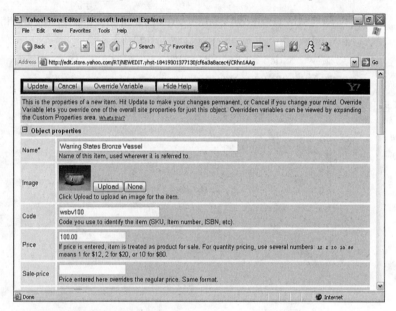

Creating Your First Product in Catalog Manager

Follow these steps to create a product using Catalog Manager:

1. In Store Manager, click on the Catalog Manager link.

2. Once you are in Catalog Manager, click on the Manage Your Item link. This will take you to the item's page, where you can add items or manage all your items as shown in Figure 9.9.

3. To add an item, click on the Add Item button. As you can see in Figure 9.10, the Add Item page is very similar to the Add Item page in Store Editor.

4. Once you are done filling out the form, click on the Save button.

You've now created a product in Catalog Manager. Although you have created a product, if you navigate to the Store Editor, you will not see the product. This is because the product has not been linked to the home page or any section. You will need to go into the content tree under the Content button on the toolbar in Store Editor to move the product to the area you want. For this reason, it is easier to use Store Editor to navigate and add your product.

FIGURE 9.9
Add Item page in Catalog Manager.

FIGURE 9.10
Add Item form in Catalog Manager.

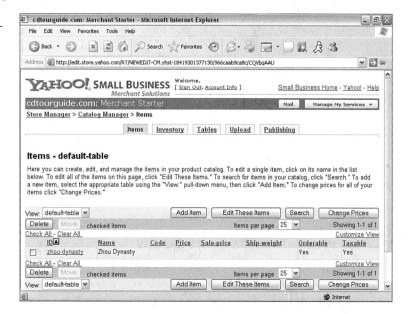

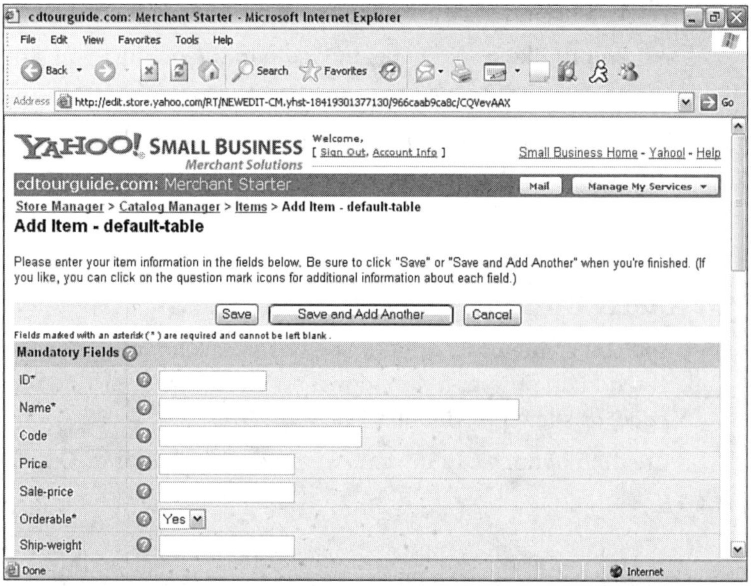

Getting to Know Catalog Manager

Since you're already in Catalog Manger, let's take a look at the five tools to help you manage your inventory.

- **Items**: Add, edit, sort, and manage all your products.
- **Tables**: Create tables to separate and group products. Tables can be used to help organize your products.
- **Inventory**: Manage the availability of your products. You can manage the inventory levels of each product.
- **Upload**: You may use a Comma-Separated Value (CSV) file to manage your products, add products, and upload them to Catalog Manager. If you have a lot of products, you may also want to look into using the CSV file to add and manage them. You can also create sections and products within sections on the fly using the CSV upload feature.
- **Publish Your Changes**: Changes to your store do not go live until you publish the catalog.

Editing Your Product in the Store Editor

One of the key benefits to editing your product in Store Editor is that you get to see exactly what the page will look like. You can edit, remove, or add product details, images, pricing, and so on. To edit your product

1. Click on Store Editor in the Store Manager.
2. Just like a web page, navigate to the product you would like to edit.
3. Click on the Edit button in the toolbar.
4. Once you are done making the changes, click on the Update button on the top of the form. This will return you to the product page with the new changes. You can preview the changes before publishing the site.

Adding Product Options

You can create order options such as size, color, and incremental pricing. Once you add an option, a drop-down menu will be displayed on your product page, as shown in Figure 9.11.

Creating options can be done in either Store Editor or Catalog Manager.

Here are two examples of how the parameters must be entered into the Options field.

Size Small Medium Large

Color Red Blue "Dark Green"

You can also set up your options for incremental pricing. For example, say you are selling T-shirts and have 3 sizes. The Small is $10, the Medium is $15, and the Large is $20. Here's how you would enter the parameters in the Options field:

Size Small Medium(+5.00) Large(+10.00)

If the customer selects Small, no incremental price is added because the product price has already been set to $10. If the customer selects Medium, a $5 charge will be added to the already set price of $10, totaling $15.

Note regarding the Options field

■ If the option has multiple words, you must enclose them between double-quotes ("Dark Green").

■ You can have more than one set of options, but they have to be separated by a line break or double space in the Options field.

■ You cannot add more than one space between the attributes.

■ HTML is not supported in the Options field.

FIGURE 9.11

Options are displayed as a drop-down menu.

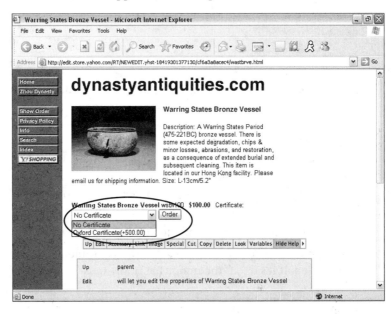

Adding Product Images

There are two ways to add product images: You can upload product images one-by-one or you can upload multiple images at the same time.

If you upload images one-by-one, you can select the Upload button shown in Figure 9.12 while editing your product or while adding a new product. After you click on the Upload button, you will be taken to another page where you can choose the location of your image to upload, as shown in Figure 9.13. This is a great option for stores with few products.

FIGURE 9.12

Image Upload button.

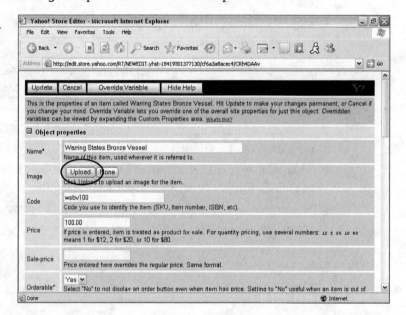

If you have a lot of products, using the multiple image upload will help you save time. This feature will upload all your images at once. How does the system know where to put the images? The name of each file must exactly match the ID of the product page. If you used the Store Editor to create your product, the product ID was created for you and you must go back into the Catalog Manager to find out what the ID is. If you used Catalog Manager to create your product, the product ID is something you entered. You can also go back into Catalog Manager to view the product ID.

The Yahoo! store supports both .jpg and .gif image formats.

For example, if your product ID is zd100, your image file name must be zd100.jpg. If it's a .gif, the image file name must be zd100.gif.

FIGURE 9.13

Image Upload
form.

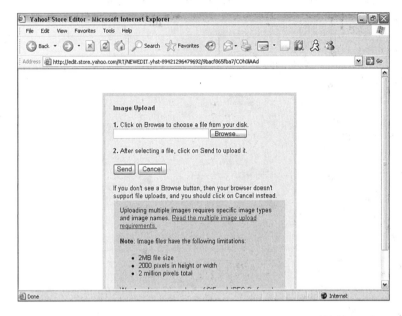

All images must be in a zip file in order to upload. This will help reduce the
file size and speed up the file upload time. You may upload as many zip files
as you wish, but only one zip file maybe uploaded at a time. If you don't
have a zip program, you may download WinZip (winzip.com) or another zip
utility program.

1. Once you have added all the image files into the zip file, click on the
   Store Editor link in the Store Manager control panel.

2. When the Store Editor homepage appears, click on the Red Triangle on
   the toolbar to display the advanced settings.

3. In the advanced settings, click on the Controls button.

4. Scroll down until you see the Multiple Image Upload link and click on
   the link, as shown in Figure 9.14.

5. Once you click on the link, a dialog box will appear where you can
   browse and upload your zip file.

Although you can see all the images you've uploaded in the Store Editor, the
changes will not be live until you publish the site.

FIGURE 9.14

Multiple Image
Upload link.

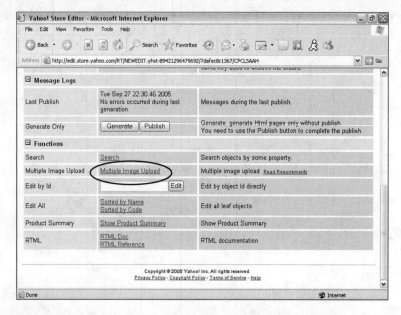

Customizing Your Page Layout and Navigation

Now that you have created a section and added products, let's take a look at
how to change the look and feel of the website. The Variables page has six
sections that control the appearance of your site. Any changes made on this
page will change the template for all your pages in your store. The best way
to figure out how each setting affects the appearance of your store is to dive
right in and test each of the settings to see whether it's what you want. If you
don't like the changes, just change back the setting.

To get to the variables page

1. Click on the Store Editor from the Store Manager.
2. Click the Store Editor link.
3. Click on the Variables button.

The six variable sections include

- **Colors and Typefaces**: Background color, link color, button color and
  size, font size and type.
- **Image Dimensions**: Image height and width for thumbnails, insets,
  and items.

- **Page Layout**: Overall page archi-tect including page width, number of columns, position of the naviga-tion menu, and elements in the head and contents area.

- **Button Properties**: Option to upload custom buttons for various buttons used throughout the site and capability to change order of the buttons in the navigation menu.

> **tip** You can also override global style properties to create page-specific styles. There is an override variable button on the Product Edit form. Navigate to the page you would like to override the variable for, and click on the Edit button on the toolbar.

- **Page Properties**: Keywords and footer content for every page.

- **Store Properties**: Commerce-related properties such as price text, cur-rency display style, and minimum dollar amount order setting.

Editing the Home Page

You can't just have a blank home page with a title. Let's take a look at editing the home page. Editing the home page is just like editing a product page.

1. From the Store Manager, click on the Store Editor link. This will take you to the home page of your site.

2. Once you are on the home page, click on the Edit button on the tool-bar.

3. This will take you to the Edit page for the home page as shown in Figure 9.15.

From the Edit page, you can customize your home page with some of the fol-lowing useful options:

- **Page Title**: Add a page title.

- **Message**: Add text to your site.

- **Page-elements**: Change the order of the elements of the page as shown in Figure 9.16.

- **Image**: Upload an image.

- **Buttons**: Change the order of the buttons in the site-wide navigation menu.

- **Columns**: Number of columns you want your products displayed is on the home page.

FIGURE 9.15

Edit form for the home page.

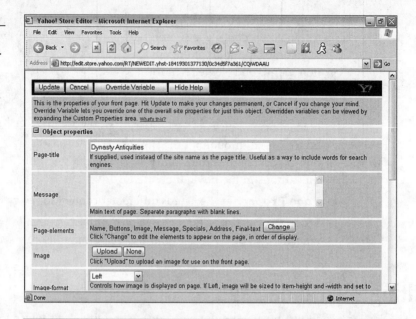

FIGURE 9.16

Page-elements change order form.

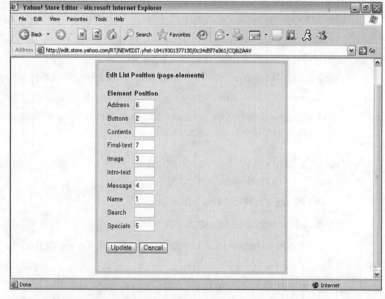

Adding Products to the Home Page

What if you have a product that's in a section and want to display it on the home page? Having products on the home page can keep the site fresh and bring attention to products, especially if they are on sale. Let's take a look at how to make a copy of the product and display it on the home page.

1. In Store Editor, navigate to the product you would like to add to the home page.

2. On the toolbar, click on the Special button. Once you click on the Special button, you will be returned to the section page.

3. Now go back to the home page and view your product.

You can add as many products as you wish to the home page. Entice repeat visitors by keeping the home page fresh with new or rotating products. Some visitors will not go past the home page if they think the site has not been updated.

Publishing Your Store

Ready to go live? It's as easy as clicking a button. Just go back to the home page of the Store Editor and click on the Publish button on the toolbar. A Publish page will show you the publishing status, as shown in Figure 9.17.

Although you can publish the store for live viewing, you will need to set up the merchant account, tax rates, shipping options, and pay methods (which credit cards you will accept). The good news is you will only need to do this once.

FIGURE 9.17
Publish Status
screen.

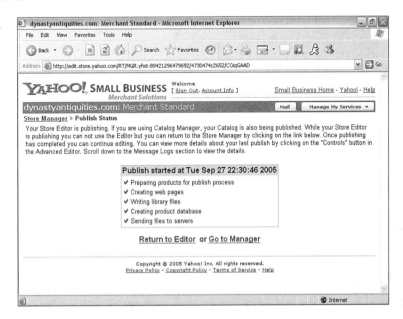

Now that you've published your storefront, the next chapter will show you how to set up your Yahoo! store order process.

Setting Up Your Yahoo!
Store Order Settings

Now that you've set up your Yahoo! store to take
orders, it's time to turn to the process of shipping them.
In Chapter 6, "Setting Up Your Business Accounts," we
spoke about choosing shipping companies and setting
up your shipping account. Will you be using UPS
(United Parcel Service), USPS (United States Postal
Service), FedEx, or a combination of different services?
Whichever method you choose, you will need to set up
those shipping options for your Yahoo! store.

Setting Up Your Shipping Options

During the checkout process, your customers will be asked to enter their shipping address and select their shipping method. The Yahoo! store order form will calculate the shipping rates and display them based on the shipping rates you set. This will also allow your customers to see their total order amount immediately. This is important because a cardinal rule of eCommerce is "never surprise your customers." In this case, provide them with the TOTAL amount of their order before you request their credit card numbers.

Shipping Manager

The Shipping Manger provides a set of tools to help you set up your shipping options. They are

- **Shipping Methods**: Add shipping methods that will be offered during the checkout process. You may add, edit, delete, or change the order of the shipping methods.
- **Shipping Rates**: Configure shipping rules based on geographic location, flat fee, and percentage or rate table.
- **Settings**: Configure general shipping calculations and UPS tools and UPS shipping settings.
- **Shipping and Order Status**: Configure and preview order status email and order confirmation emails.
- **Shipping and Tax Test**: Test shipping rules with sample data based on tax tables before publishing to the live store.

To access the Shipping Manager

1. From the Manage My Services control panel, click on Store Manager.
2. In Store Manager, click on Shipping Manager under the Order Settings column.

Setting Your Shipping Methods

Once you decide which shipping methods to offer, you will need to add those options to the shipping methods form. You can add general default shipping options such as Downloadable, Ground, Air, Federal Express, and First Class Mail as provided by Merchant Solutions or add your own custom method.

During the checkout process, a drop-down menu will display all of the shipping options you provide, as seen in Figure 10.1.

To add shipping methods

1. From the Manage My Services control panel, click on Store Manager.

2. In Store Manager, click on Shipping Manager under the Order Settings column.

3. In Shipping Manager, click on Shipping Methods.

4. Once you are on the Shipping Methods page, click on the Edit Methods button to add shipping methods.

tip If you are charging a flat fee for shipping, you may want to consider adding the shipping cost as part of your shipping option title. Your customers will want to know how much each shipping method costs. This will reduce phone calls, tech support emails, and customer hesitation when ordering.

Once you have finished adding your shipping methods, you will need to configure your shipping rates. To view a free online video of how to add shipping methods, go to www.MyEcommerceSuccess.com.

FIGURE 10.1
Shipping options are displayed in a drop-down menu during the checkout process.

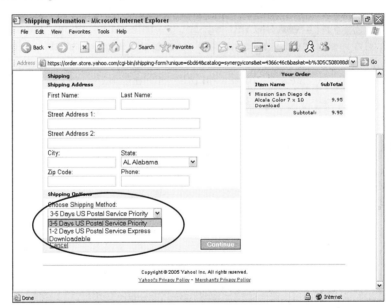

Configuring Shipping Rates

To set shipping rates, you will need to create shipping rules. You can charge a flat fee, charge a percentage of the order amount, or use a rate table that is based on weight, order amount, or number of items sold. You may also include an additional fee to cover handling cost. For example, if the shipping cost for a T-shirt is $3.95 for USPS priority mail, you may want to add $1.05 for handling and charge a flat $5 for shipping.

Also, keep in mind that shipping companies such as UPS determine shipping rates based on zones. For example, it will cost more to send a package from California to New York than from New York to Boston. If you are planning on using UPS, UPS has an online tool that will allow you customers to view real-time shipping rates during the checkout process.

Once you select your shipping methods, you can create shipping rate rules. There are five sequential steps to create each rule.

1. **Select Location**: You can specify which country, state, and ZIP codes this rule will apply to, as shown in Figure 10.2.

2. **Select Method(s)**: Which shipping method(s) this rule will apply to.

3. **Rule Type**: Whether the shipping charge be based on a flat rate, a percentage of order amount, or a rate table.

4. **Rate Details**: The details and exact amount of for each rule type.

5. **Override Setting**: The Override setting allows you to apply only one rule even though an order matches other existing rules. For example, you may have a flat shipping fee for all of the United States, but offer free shipping for all orders from California.

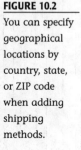

FIGURE 10.2

You can specify geographical locations by country, state, or ZIP code when adding shipping methods.

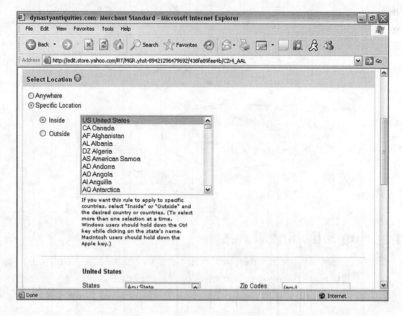

To add shipping rates

1. From the Manage My Services control panel, click on Store Manager.

2. In Store Manager, click on Shipping Manager under the Order Settings column.

3. In Shipping Manager, click on Shipping Rates.

4. Once you are on the Shipping Rates page, click on the Add Rule button to add shipping rates.

5. Follow the five steps as described earlier to add your shipping rates.

Using UPS Shipping Tools

Planning on using UPS (United Parcel Service)? UPS Online Tools is integrated with Yahoo! Merchant Solutions at no extra charge. With UPS Online Tools, you can process shipments, auto-insert tracking numbers into orders, receive real-time rates and auto-populate shipping labels without leaving the Store Manager. Using UPS Online Tools will help streamline your shipping process and save you time. Your customers will also be able to track their orders anytime via the UPS website. This will reduce emails and phone calls asking, "When will I receive my order?" and improve customer service.

In order to use the UPS shipping tools, you must apply for a UPS account. To register for an account, go to the Shipping Manager in Store Manager and click the Register to Use UPS Online Tools link. This will take you through the registration process.

Using Checkout Manager to Customize the Checkout Pages

During the checkout process, customers will be taken to a page where they will be asked for their shipping info, billing info, and credit card information. Merchant Solutions provides a default generic order form as seen in Figure 10.3. But what if you would like to carry your brand and "look and feel" throughout the checkout process? You can customize the checkout pages by adding custom HTML to the header, sidebar, and footer. Checkout Manager will also allow you to upload custom CSS (Cascading Style Sheets) files. CSS will allow you to define colors, fonts, layouts, and other aspects of the document presentation. It's extremely useful when you want to make global changes to certain styles defined by CSS. Customizing the checkout page will allow you to match the site design throughout the ordering process.

It's a good idea to customize pages like this where available to give your store-front the unique look or "brand" of your company. This re-enforces in the mind of your customer your uniqueness, how you differ from your competition, and a way to remember you when your customers want to buy your products or services in the future.

To access Checkout Manager

1. From the Manage My Services Control Panel, click on the Store Manager link.

2. In Store Manager, click on the Checkout Manager link under the Order Settings column.

FIGURE 10.3

Merchant Solutions provides a generic checkout page. But, you can customize the checkout pages with your "look and feel" by using the Checkout Manager.

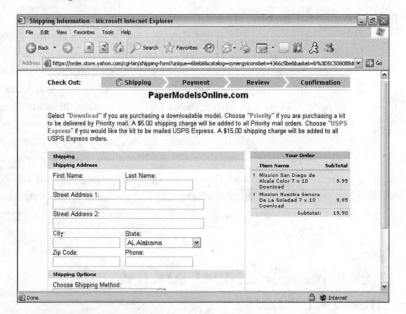

Using Inventory Management

Merchant Solutions has an inventory management system that lets you set stock levels for your products. You can even use different options for different products. For example, you can set separate stock levels for a T-shirt that is available in multiple colors. You might have 35 black T-shirts and only 20 white T-shirts available. You can also set the system to send you an email alert once the inventory reaches a certain inventory threshold. The alert will give you time to restock your inventory.

With inventory management, you can also set the shopping cart to display the number of available units when customers add the item to their shopping cart, as shown in Figure 10.4.

FIGURE 10.4

When inventory management is enabled, you can display the available units of a particular product when the customer adds an item to the shopping cart.

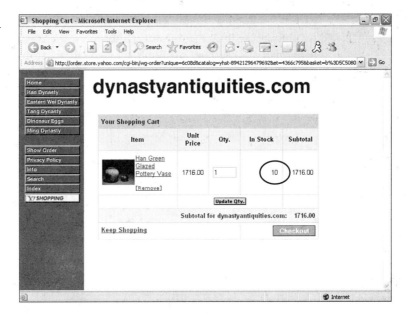

What happens when you run out of stock on a particular product before you are able to restock your inventory? You can set the shopping cart to display a message that the particular product is currently unavailable. Instead of pulling the product from the store, you can just display this message. This will let your customer know that the product is still being offered, but is currently unavailable.

Setting Up Inventory Management

1. In Store Manager, click on Configure Inventory under Order Settings.

2. There are three inventory option choices: None, Real-time Inventory, and Database Inventory. Real-time Inventory will use an inventory script running on your own server. For this example, we will be using Database Inventory because it can be configured using Merchant Solutions. Once you select Database Inventory and click the Modify Settings button, the page will refresh with additional configuration options.

There are two additional sections when you select Database Inventory: Alerts and Settings.

- **Alerts**: Send email alerts, set alert thresholds, and set the time and frequency of the alert emails.

- **Settings**: Allow customer to see the availability or quantity of the product, set default inventory quantity, and set whether quantity can exceed availability. If you select No for the Quantity Can Exceed Availability setting, the following message will be displayed: "None: Requested quantity not available for some items at this time."

After you have configured all your settings, you will then need to input the inventory level for each of your product.

Setting Inventory Levels

1. Click on the Inventory link under Process in Store Manager.
2. Click the Edit button. The page will refresh and a Quantity field box will appear for each item.
3. Enter the current inventory level for each item as shown in Figure 10.5 and click the Save button.

FIGURE 10.5

You can enter current inventory levels in the Quantity field box.

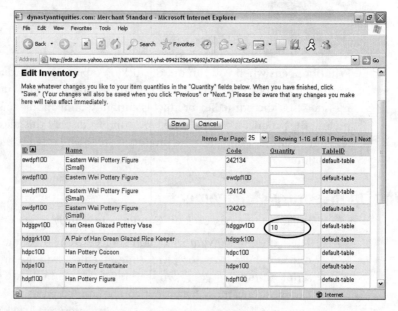

Setting Inventory Levels for Product Options

Inventory levels can be set for product options but will require a unique code for each option. For example, if you are selling T-shirts that are available in three different sizes, each size will require its own unique code. Once you assign each option a code, the product option will then be displayed in the inventory listing. If you do not assign a code for each option, you will only be able to set an inventory level for the product, and not the options.

Assigning Unique Codes to Product Options

1. From the Store Manager, click on the Catalog Manager link under the Edit column.

2. From Catalog Manger, click on the Manage Your Items link. A list of your products will be displayed. You can view up to 100 products at a time.

3. Click on the product link you would like to add option codes to.

4. Scroll down until you see the Options field. Your options must be defined before you can enter your option codes. Once you have defined your options, click on the Enter Individual Items Code link underneath the Options field box, as seen in Figure 10.6.

5. A page will appear with blank code field boxes next to your specified options, as shown in Figure 10.7. Make sure you select the corresponding option from the drop-down menu. The drop-down menu defaults to the first product option defined in the items page. Once you enter your new options code, click on the Save and Continue button.

Once you have completed entering the options code, you can then go back to the Inventory page in Catalog Manager and enter the inventory level.

FIGURE 10.6

To enter options codes, click on the Enter Individual Items Code link underneath the Options field box.

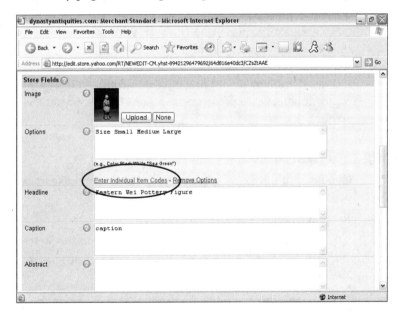

FIGURE 10.7
Enter product
option codes in
the blank fields
next to each
option.

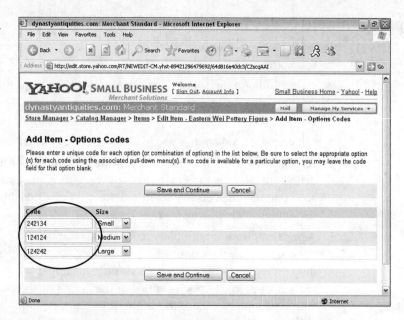

Setting Up Your Merchant Account

In Chapter 6, we discussed the need for a merchant account. A merchant
account is required to accept all major credit cards including Visa, Master
Card, American Express, and Discover. With Merchant Solutions, you can
choose to apply for Paymentech (paymentech.com)—Yahoo! Merchant
Solutions's preferred provider—or any other compatible First Data Merchant
Services (FDMS) merchant account (fdms.com). Yahoo! store uses FDMS as a
payment gateway to process transactions from your store with your merchant
account.

Applying for Paymentech

If you do not have a merchant account and would like to use Paymentech,
you may apply online.

To apply online

1. Go to Pay Methods under Order Settings in the Store Manager.

2. Once the Payment Method page appears, click on the Apply for
   Paymentech link.

3. Complete the online application form as shown in Figure 10.8.

FIGURE 10.8

Paymentech merchant account online application form.

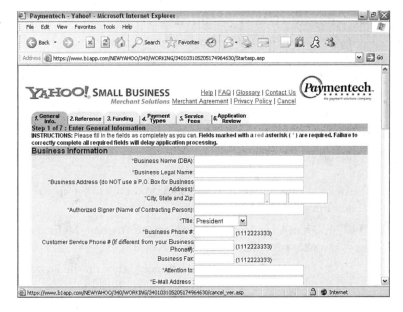

In order to apply for a Paymentech merchant account, you will need the following information.

- Business contact information
- Federal tax ID number (or Social Security # if not incorporated)
- Third-party fulfillment provider contact info (if applicable)
- Current credit card processor contact info (if applicable)
- Business owner and bank reference information
- Funding information (bank routing numbers for your business's checking account)
- Land line based telephone number for business. A cellular telephone number will not be accepted.
- Application status will be sent via email. A valid/active email address is required to process the application.

Once you complete the online application, it will take approximately five working days to process your application. You may also email Paymentech at IssVirtualCreditApps@firstdata.com to check up on your application status.

Using Your Own Merchant Account

If you already have a merchant account or would like to use a merchant account provider other than Paymentech, you will need to request the following information from your merchant account provider.

- Name of merchant bank
- Merchant number
- MID (Merchant identification)
- Terminal identification

The following instructions will show you how to set up your own merchant account with Merchant Solutions.

1. From Store Manager, click on the Payment Methods link under the Order Settings column.
2. From the Payment Methods page, click on the Payment Processing and Setup Management link as shown in Figure 10.9.
3. Click on the Setup Existing Merchant Account link.
4. Fill out the form with the information from your Merchant Account as shown in Figure 10.10, and then click the Setup button.

FIGURE 10.9

You can add your own Merchant Account via the Set up Processing Through FDMS link on the Payment Methods page.

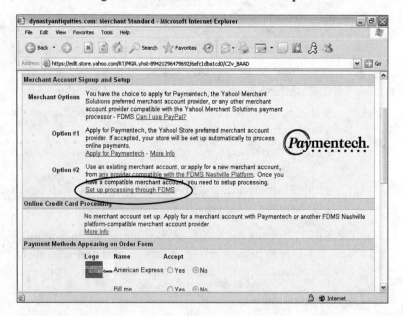

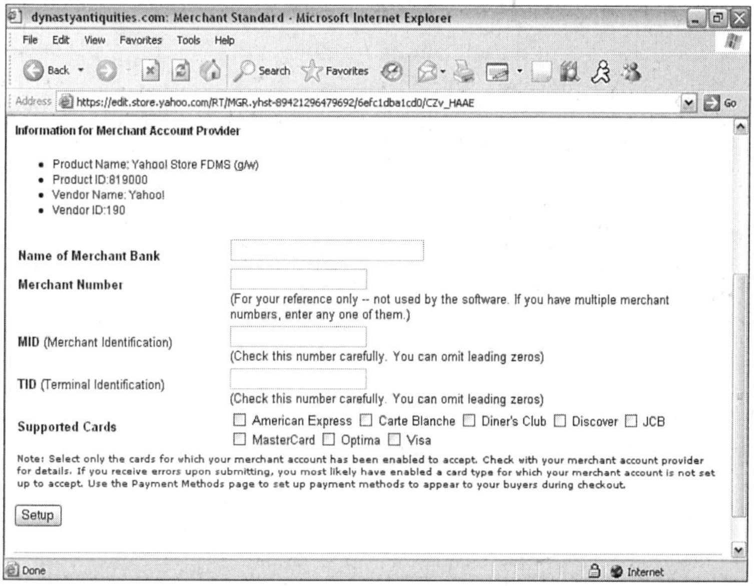

FIGURE 10.10

The name of the merchant bank, merchant number, merchant identification, and terminal identification are required to enable your own merchant account with Merchant Solutions.

Payment Methods

So which credit cards will you accept online? Will it be Visa, MasterCard, Discover, JCB, American Express, or another credit card? Will you accept them all or a combination? In order to accept credit cards, you first must have a merchant account. Once you obtain a merchant account, you will need to find out which credit cards the account allows you to accept. If you are using Paymentech, you will be automatically set up to accept Visa, MasterCard, and Diner's Club payments.

Credit Card Fees

Every time an order is placed, a fee is imposed by the merchant account provider and is paid by the merchant. The fee is a percentage of the total sale, which includes any shipping and handling. As mentioned in Chapter 6, the percentage can range between 2% and 3% for Visa, MasterCard, and Discover, and between 3% and 5% for American Express. So if your discount rate for a Visa card is 2%, your Merchant Bank will take 2%—or $2 of that $100 customer purchase—and deposit the remainder in your bank account. The actual percentage will depend on your type of business, average sale, and/or monthly volume.

The following is a list of a few credit card companies and their phone numbers for you to contact regarding their fees.

tip Contact your merchant account provider and ask which credit card payment types their system can process. They may also have online applications on their website to apply for other credit card companies.

- American Express/Optima (americanexpress.com): (800) 528-5200
- Diners Club/Carte Blanche (dinersclub.com): (800) 525-7376
- Novus/Discover (discover.com): (800) 347-2000
- JCB (jcbcorporate.com): (800) 366-4522

Accepting Other Types of Credit Cards

For all other credit cards, you will need to contact the credit card company you would like to use and apply for an account. You will then need to contact your merchant account provider once you get approval from that particular credit card. Once that is set up, you can then go into the Payment Methods form to add the new credit cards you would like to accept so that they will appear on the checkout payment form.

Accepting PayPal

What if you don't want a merchant account or if you don't meet the requirements for a merchant account and would like to use PayPal (paypal.com) as your payment method instead? Yahoo! Merchant Solutions is also integrated with PayPal Express. Customers to your store can have an option to pay via a PayPal account or use their credit cards to pay through PayPal. With PayPal, there are no monthly fees or setup fees. Using PayPal can be an alternative for hobbyists. It doesn't require a corporate account or EIN. You can run PayPal off your personal debit, checking, or credit card.

PayPal, an eBay company (ebay.com), has more than 78 million members worldwide and is available in 56 countries and regions. PayPal was started as a secure and inexpensive solution to send money from one individual to another online. Now PayPal offers solutions to accept credit cards, bank transfers, and debit cards on your website and via email.

For more information, please visit store.yahoo.com.

Setting Up Tax Rates

If your product or service requires you to charge sales tax, you may set up tax rate rules in the Tax Rates page under Order Settings in the Store Manager control panel. There are two options for the type of tax rule: percentage or flat fee. Most taxes are percentage based. You may set up tax rules based on country, state, or ZIP code.

If you are setting up United States tax rules for the first time, you may want to consider using the Auto Setup Wizard. The wizard will allow you to automatically fill in the values for each state's taxes. This will save you a tremendous amount of time by not having to find out what each state's sales tax is and enter each rate one-by-one.

To use Auto Setup Wizard to set up tax rates

1. Click on the Tax Rates link under Order Settings in Store Manager.

2. Click on the Auto Setup Wizard link, as shown in Figure 10.11.

3. After you have selected your location, click the Next button.

4. In the scroll menu, highlight the states you would like to charge sales tax for and click the Done button. To select multiple states, hold down the Control button on your keyboard and click on each state.

5. The Tax Rate page will appear with your new tax rule(s), as shown in Figure 10.12.

FIGURE 10.11

Using the Auto Setup Wizard to set up your tax rates will automatically add the rates for each state.

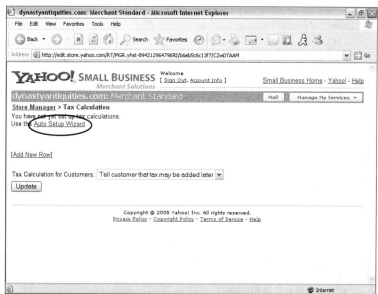

FIGURE 10.12

FIGURE 10.12

Rates for each state have automatically been set using the Auto Setup Wizard.

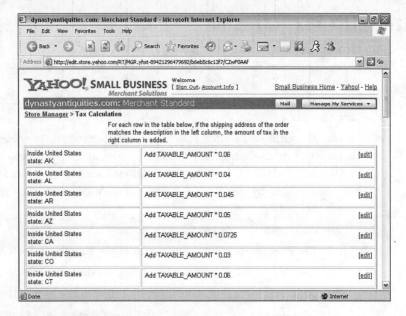

Setting Up Your Email Accounts

Yahoo! Mail Business Edition comes with every Merchant Solutions account. Each account includes up to 100 individual email accounts. Unlike other email programs, each email account has the capability to send and receive large file attachments up to 10 megabytes.

Not only can you set up an email POP account and use your preferred email client such as Outlook, Eudora, or Entourage (on the Mac), but you can also set up a webmail Account to send and receive email via any web browser. POP is an email protocol that allows you to manage, retrieve, and compose messages using your own email client. Being able to access your email via any web browser will come in handy, especially if you are on the road. You can still receive orders, process orders, and stay in touch with your customers via an Internet kiosk or at an internet café.

You can add accounts, edit accounts, set up email forwarding, and manage all email accounts via the Email Control Panel.

To add an email account:

1. From the Manage My Services control panel, click on the Email Control Panel link.

2. Click on the Create Address button.

3. Enter the email address you would like to create and then click on the Create Mailbox button, as shown in Figure 10.13.

4. You will then be given an option to select POP and webmail access or a POP Email Only mailbox. If you would like to be able to send and receive emails via a web browser and your email software program such as Outlook, select the POP and Webmail option. Once you make your selection, click on the Continue button.

5. A page will appear asking you if you would like to print the instructions on how to activate the new email account or have the instructions sent to another email address. If you are setting up an email address for another person, you can have the instruction email sent to that person if they have another email account.

Email Settings for POP and SMTP Setup

Incoming Mail (POP3) Server:	pop.bizmail.yahoo.com
Outgoing Mail (SMTP) Server:	smtp.bizmail.yahoo.com
Account Name/Sign-in Name:	you@yourcompany.com
Email Address:	you@yourcompany.com
Password:	Your Yahoo! ID password

FIGURE 10.13

You can create email accounts via the Email Control Panel.

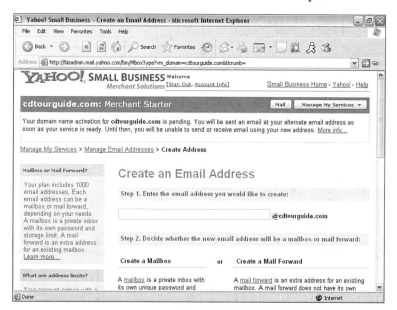

Receiving Orders via Email

Once your email account is set up, you can receive orders via email automatically every time an order is placed. You can also have Yahoo! send a copy of your email order notifications to multiple email accounts. This comes in handy when you have more than one person involved with processing and fulfilling orders. You can have one email notification sent to the shipping department and another one to the accounting department for processing. Email order notification can be sent immediately or at a certain time, and can be sent in different formats such as plain text, Adobe PDF attachment, QuickBooks, and XML.

To access the order system settings, click on the Order Emails link under Order Settings in Store Manager. From here you can enter the email addresses you want the orders sent to, the time you want it delivered, and the format you want it in, as shown in Figure 10.14.

FIGURE 10.14
Order system
settings control
panel.

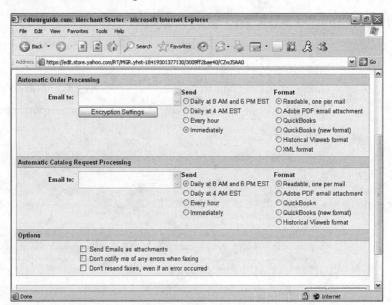

Publishing Your Order Settings

Once you have configured all your store's order settings, you will need to publish your changes. Publishing the order settings is different from publishing your website product pages, as described in Chapter 9, "Creating Your Yahoo! Store." Publishing the order settings will only publish the following tools:

- Checkout Manager
- Risk Tools
- Pay Methods
- Foreign Orders

- Shipping Methods
- Tax Rates
- Inventory Settings

To publish order settings

1. In Store Manager, click on the Publish Order Settings link under the Order Settings column.
2. When the Order Settings page appears, click on the Publish button.

Now that you've configured and published all your Yahoo! store order settings and are ready for business, let's take a look at basic marketing promotions, including how to generate traffic for free.

Part IV

Launching Your Yahoo! Store

CHAPTER

11

Basic Marketing—Promoting Your Yahoo! Store for Free

"**B**uild it and they will come"' may have worked for Kevin Costner in *Field of Dreams*, but it holds little water when it comes to attracting visitors to your Yahoo! store. You may have the best designed and executed eCommerce storefront on the Net, but unless shoppers know you exist, all your work is for naught.

In this and the two chapters that follow, we'll show you the basics of promoting that great little Yahoo! store that you have successfully designed and implemented. In this chapter, we'll focus on how to promote it for free.

The old saying goes "There's no such thing as a free lunch." But that's not necessarily true online, for there's another saying from Thomas Edison: "Success is 1% inspiration and 99% perspiration." If you're willing to spend your time but not your money and ready to sweat a little, there are ways to market your storefront for free.

Start in Meatspace

Beforeyou venture into the online world of free marketing, you should start with what can be done offline to assist in the promotion of your storefront. Just because you have a virtual company doesn't mean you should ignore the real world. Or in the lexicon of the Internet, *meatspace*. There are opportunities to use the real world to market your storefront, and with no extra cost!

First of all, spread that URL of yours around. Before you reach for your mouse to market online, make sure you sprinkle your URL on every stitch of printed material that leaves your office. And include your company's email address, too.

Place both your URL and your company email address on all literature, collateral, business cards, letterheads, invoices, and the like. Also mention your URL on any and all media advertising you do. This also includes both the Yellow Pages and Business White Pages. Also, if your business uses POS (Point of Sale) packaging and/or display (such as at trade shows), you need to incorporate your URL and main email address on them, too.

You spent good money for traditional media—make it count.

Next, spread the word.

Do you belong to any business associations? Are you a member of your local Chamber of Commerce? If so, contact them and ask that your website be added to their listings both online and off. Contact sites that service a regional area and ask that your site be listed with them. Many will comply. If they ask for a listing fee, move on to another organization.

Finally, stuff it!

There's plenty of empty space in your shipping boxes. Here's an opportunity to use meatspace to promote your site, exclusive specials, and immediate resales, as well as to cross promote and upsell.

Consider this: One of the best times to make a sale is immediately after a customer purchases from you. This is a well-known fact in catalog sales. Make a purchase from a successful catalog house and in your shipping box you'll find several offers for additional products or exclusive time-sensitive offers. So toss in several pieces of printed material hawking a new product, or give a discount or free shipping on their next order.

It only takes a minute to toss the flyers in the box before it's sealed, and it could result in additional sales.

Using Yahoo! Properties to Promote for Free

Keep in mind that unless you have substantial resources (or happen to be a relative of Bill Gates), promoting your new eBusiness takes a lot of hard work and time to see results. So make the most of your time with these basic grass-roots marketing strategies.

Promotion does not mean advertising. So, before you go out and spend a bundle of money advertising, start your marketing first on a grassroots level. Yahoo! has a set of free promotion tools that you can use to help your grass-roots marketing endeavors.

Sow Your Participation and Reap Site Visitors

One of the best ways to get the word out about your company and what it offers is to join in the community gabfest that's on the Internet. By monitoring and participating in newsgroups and discussion lists, you have the opportunity to respond to potential customers and promote your product or service. Participation in newsgroups, discussion boards, industry appropriate blogs, and chat rooms on the Net is a great way to gain visibility for your eBusiness, and it's free!

> # caution
>
> ### Newsgroup Etiquette
>
> You *should not* post an advertisement stating that you are open for business. That's not how it works, and if you do you will be flamed for spamming the list. To avoid this, first read the postings of the group for a few weeks to get the general nature and feel of the list. This is called *lurking*.

The trick is to choose the right community participation vehicles and make a contribution to the discussion. Let's take newsgroups and discussion boards for example. Before the birth of the World Wide Web, online marketers relied heavily on newsgroups. Although they have waned as a marketing vehicle, they still are an important free promotional resource.

A good place to start is Yahoo! Groups at groups.yahoo.com (see Figure 11.1). With a little time and energy, you can find Yahoo! groups and newsgroups on the Net where your product and expertise can lead to visitors and sales. Though Yahoo! Groups is not a discussion board as such, you can post messages to the group to gain visibility for your business. A great place to find actual newsgroups is at Google Groups at groups.google.com. It's the easiest way to navigate the Net's newsgroups without the use of a newsreader program.

Make sure you read the FAQs (frequently asked questions) for the lists you want to participate in. The FAQs will tell you what you can and cannot post to the group. You might find that some groups do allow you to post a message that reads like an ad. Remember, what you're looking for is an opportunity to respond to individual posts for help or enter into an ongoing discussion where your product or service might add to the discussion. If done right, when it's time for those on the newsgroup to buy, they'll remember you first.

FIGURE 11.1

Yahoo! Groups is a good resource for finding mailing lists that relate to your product or service.

For example, if you sell home alarms and are participating in a Yahoo! Groups home security discussion group (groups.yahoo.com/group/Security-Systems/), be prepared to offer advice and news about the security industry in general and perhaps home security devices in particular. If you have a legal service, offer to answer specific questions on legal issues.

In addition to Yahoo! Groups, there are good discussion board sites that have numerous discussion boards on just about any topic that you can monitor and participate in. The best of the lot is Delphi Forums. Delphi Forums, at delphiforums.com (see Figure 11.2), is one of the largest discussion boards on the Net and has more than 500,000 individual discussion forums to participate in.

tip Don't Forget to Tell Them Who You Are

Remember to add your signature or *sig* file to each message you post so people can contact you or visit your web store off the board or list.

There are three elements of a sig file that will pack the punch of a promotional ad. The first is a good tag line that conveys your value proposition and summarizes the benefit of your product, answering the question "Why should I care? (WIIFM)." Second, provide a direct link to your offer. And third, provide multiple ways to contact you. Remember to keep your sig file to no more than 4–5 lines.

FIGURE 11.2

You can access
and post to
more than
500,000 individ-
ual discussion
forums at Delphi
Forums.

Discussion Lists and Live Chat

Besides newsgroups and discussion boards on the Net, there are email discussion lists. A discussion list is the email equivalent of discussion boards or
newsgroups. But instead of posting your message on a website, you send an
email to the list. Every Yahoo! Group has the capability to send emails to the
entire group with just a click of the Send button.

So how do you build such a list using Yahoo! Groups?

When visitors come to your storefront, ask if they would like to be placed on
your mailing list. If so, ask them to submit their email address to you, and
enter them as members of your Yahoo! Group. This is not only important for
building an email list, but also for your blog. We'll discuss blogging in the
next section. A good resource that takes the day-to-day hassle out of managing your mailing list is Constant Contact at www.ConstantContact.com. They
have a very inexpensive, easy-to-use, and effective system for collecting, managing, and conducting email marketing campaigns.

By and large, interactive discussion lists usually offer better quality discussions than newsgroups and discussion boards. These discussions are in the
form of emails and show up in your mailbox every day. When you want to
post to a list you have subscribed to, you send an email to the list and the list
sends your message out to everyone who has subscribed to it.

Besides Yahoo! Groups, you can locate other discussion lists that fit your market niche at Lsoft (lsoft.com/lists/listref.html). It has the CataList (see Figure
11.3), the official catalog of LISTSERV lists on the Net. CataList has more than

tens of thousands of public discussion lists that you can subscribe to. At Lsoft you can search lists by interest or host country, view lists with 10,000 subscribers or more, or view lists with 1,000 subscribers or more. Another good source is Liszt at liszt.com. It has thousands of email discussion lists in dozens of topic categories to choose from.

FIGURE 11.3

CataList has more than tens of thousands of public discussion lists that you can subscribe to.

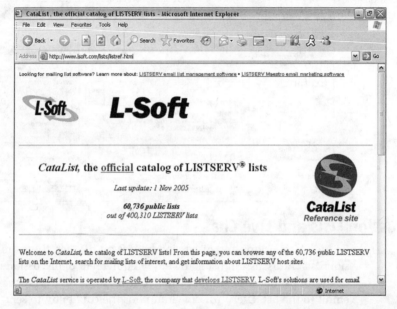

Finally, don't forget the live chat rooms on the Net. They can be a great free source of promotion for your new storefont. And besides, you'll be talking directly, and live, to potential customers. Some of the best chat rooms for online businesses can be found at Delphi Forums Chat at delphiforums.com.

Learn to Blog

A somewhat new horse in the promotion stable is blogging. The word *blog* is a contraction of *web log*. A blog is updated frequently—many are updated daily—by one or a few people who post a

> **tip**
>
> ### Become a Trusted Authority
>
> It is more important to be a quality addition to the group or list than to pounce on every opportunity to plug a product or service. If you develop a reputation as an **authority** with the group, when you do give recommendations, they will carry more weight. If you just plug products without building a reputation, group members will just see your comments as ads and not recommendations. Also, if you are an authority, group members may begin to solicit your advice on products directly.

continuous stream of personal commentary and links, writing informally and in conversational style.

So what does that mean to you? It's a free alternate way to market your store-front.

Building a personal relationship with your customers is the prime way of keeping them loyal and buying from you over and over again. And blogging is built for personal communications. Acting as a commentator, have your blog comment on your industry, products, and services. Give down-to-earth one-to-one personal observations speaking directly to your customers and prospects as if they were face-to-face. You can also link to your newsletter and promote it on your website. You might be pleasantly surprised at the response from your customers and prospects.

Yahoo! has just introduced a blogging tool in the Yahoo! 360 community. With Yahoo! 360, you can create your own blog or online journal and add photos. You can even post photos and text messages from your mobile phone. As a business tool, it's a great way to keep your customers informed about what's going on with your company or industry. Providing a frequently updated blog will not only help generate traffic, but also create customer loy-alty and position you as an industry authority.

Yahoo! is also adding blogs to its Yahoo! news index. What does that mean for you? Keeping your blogs updated with current news or keyword searches will help generate traffic to your blog. All you need to create a blog is a web browser. No specialized software is needed. To get started creating your blog, go to 360.yahoo.com.

Another free blogging tool can be found at blogger.com. This is a very popu-lar tool that can get your blog up and running in minutes.

Publish an Email Newsletter

Publishing an electronic newsletter is one of the most cost effective ways of promoting your storefront, and by using Yahoo! Groups, you can do it for free. And here's the kicker—you can send an email newsletter to your prospects and customers who sign up for your Yahoo! Group in either plain text or HTML format. That means you can place images of your product in your newsletter.

Think about it. You have a list of people who have voluntarily given you their email addresses and asked that they be kept informed about your business, your industry, and the product or service you offer. But remember the flip side of this permission-based relationship: Your visitors and customers have signed up for your newsletter to be informed, so don't use it to hit them over the head with nothing but advertising for your products or services. Also, publishing a newsletter comes with the price of responsibility to produce a newsletter every period.

Deliver useful information and you'll be surprised how many prospects and customers you can build relationships with and encourage to return to your site. It might take considerable time and some sweat to write and execute a quality newsletter, but the payoff in customer retention and response can be huge.

Now, this is important. When a subscriber signs up for your newsletter, that's what he or she expects to get—*news*. Your subscribers asked to be sent news, not offers. If you pull the old switcheroo on them by sending them an email filled with nothing but product or service promotions, they will only see what your attempts at relationship-building really are: a cheap way to promote your wares. If you want to send 100% product or service promotional emails, make that a separate email list and get permission from customers and prospects to send it to them.

So what's the difference between a promotional email and newsletter? First, it's in the percentage, and second, in the format.

Let's take percentage first. Your newsletter should have at least 80–90% news, consisting of links to third-party information and articles about the product or service you sell and the concerns of your prospects and customers. That is, your newsletter should contain information your subscribers can use, such as movie, book, or music reviews or upcoming updates to the product they've purchased. You also can enhance your reputation and get business through well-written articles in your product or service subject area.

Customers and prospects are always looking for information that can help them use or purchase the products and services they need. This is where you can shine as a helper and facilitator for your clients. Here's a tip: Think like a soap opera writer and write a series of articles that build on each other. At the end of each one, include a "teaser" promoting what comes next. You also can archive these information-type newsletters on your site, adding more content for shoppers to view when they visit.

The remainder of the newsletter should be about your company and its products or service. In other words, 80–90% of your newsletter should be focused on your subscribers' needs, the rest on yours.

Now on to format.

First, how long should your newsletter be? If you have valuable information to say in your newsletter, don't be afraid of its length. Give subscribers valuable information on a topic they're passionate about and they'll read every word. Besides, your newsletter should have as many of these elements as possible:

- A welcome
- News to use
- Customer-focused news
- Feature article or tips
- Tell a friend
- Subscribe and unsubscribe instructions
- A link to your website

First the welcome. Thank your readers for subscribing and give a quick summary of what is contained in the current issue. And remember you're speaking to one, and only one, person at a time. Write as if you're speaking only to him or her and keep the tone causal and personal.

Second is news they can use. Link to current news items about your product or service and market niche. If you're selling gaming software, for example, give brief news summaries of articles that review the latest games and the gaming industry, then link to them in your newsletter.

Third, if you're a B2B—businesses-to-business—why not profile one of your customers in each newsletter? You might even explain how your services or product helped them solve a business problem. One-on-one interviews are another way to spotlight your customer and the challenges your industry faces. These interviews could be made with industry experts in your niche. For example, what competitive pressure is your industry facing or what's the future of your product or service?

Fourth, write a short useful feature, or better yet, supply a series of tips that your customers can use. Think about packaging your message. People like to think in terms of numbers. Package your message in terms of "The 10 Tips for ..." or "The 6 Secrets of ..." or "The Seven Mistakes of ...." Another way to package your content is in the form of "Did You Know" or "Frequently Asked Questions." Also, try to get guest authors to write an article for you. It's a good way to build credibility and have someone else do the work for you.

Fifth, ask readers to tell a friend about your newsletter. If they like what they read, ask them to forward the newsletter to friends, family, and colleagues, and build in the referral code in your newsletter to do it.

Sixth, make sure you supply simple and easy instructions on how to unsubscribe, and to those who have been forwarded the newsletter by friends, family, or colleagues, how to subscribe. And finally, make sure to provide a link in your newsletter to your website.

Should you send your newsletter as plain text or in HTML?

Many of the popular email programs today can read an HTML-formatted email. An HTML-formatted email appears, when opened, as a web page instead of lines of simple ASCII text. That means you can display images, photographs, colors, and graphics in your email, which makes for a much richer experience for your reader. But remember, many people are still on dial-up. That means it will take a 1 megabyte email one hour to download. So consider the size of your HTML newsletter when creating it, or write it in text with a link to the HTML version.

More advanced email marketers who need to track their email campaign's success might consider using Campaigner, powered by GOT. We'll talk more about Campaigner in the next chapter. Campaigner will allow you generate real-time reports with open rates and even show which customer clicked on which link or advertisement. The detailed reports will help you determine what your readers' interests are. This will help you refine and improve your email newsletter. You can sign-up for Campaigner in the Store Manager under the Promote column.

Other email newsletter software companies

- **Constant Contact**: constantcontact.com
- **BlueHornet**: bluehornet.com
- **Exact Target**: exacttarget.com

So there we are. If you follow the suggestions in this chapter, you are well on your way to promoting your online storefront, without spending a penny to start. In the next chapter, we'll discuss how to use Internet search engines to further promote your company as well as the marketing value of your eCommerce website statistics.

Search Engine Optimization and Listing

In Chapter 11, "Basic Marketing—Promoting Your Yahoo! Store for Free," we discussed how to generate traffic using email newsletters, newsgroups, blogs, and other traditional media to promote your site. Now let's discuss how to generate traffic from search engines. So why are search engines so popular and why are so many websites spending an enormous amount of money for top placement? The answer is simple: because it works! Search engines are usually the first thing a consumer uses to find information or a product. Some online companies even rely solely on search engine traffic as the only source of revenue. Having and maintaining excellent ranking can make or break companies overnight.

Registering Your Store at Search Engines and Directories

Billions of searches are performed on search engines each month. According to the Nielsen/NetRatings global index estimates, there are more than 450 million at-home Internet users on the planet. In May 2005, the average user went online 32 times; spent 26 hours, 28 minutes surfing the Internet; visited 65 websites; and viewed 1,203 web pages. The average time spent on one page was 43 seconds. These numbers will only continue to grow as computers become less expensive, broadband connectivity become more widely available, and the Internet becomes more available in other countries.

So with more than 5 billion web pages on the Internet and growing, how will consumers find your site? Although you may be competing with a million other web pages, it's not impossible to get top ranking. It sounds logical that every web page would be optimized for search engines, but not everyone is doing it. Also, search engines are constantly changing their formulas on how they rank web pages. Your web page could be number one on a particular keyword search one day and be 100 pages deep the next. It is very important to keep up with the constant changes and continuously work on your search engine optimization and marketing strategy in order to maintain or improve your ranking.

So what are the differences between search engines and directories?

Free Info   Download the free informative article titled "10 Ways to Drive Customers Away from Your Site" at www.MyEcommerceSuccess.com.

Search Engines

A search engine spiders or crawls your site, scans your content, and then indexes your web pages. It's done by specialized software. It scans your website and other pages or sites linked from your site. If you have a link on another website that has been crawled, it is likely your site will also be crawled and indexed. The search engine takes all that information and stores it in a database.

So who are the "big dogs" that you need to pay close attention to? The top five search engines account for the majority of the market. You can also submit your site to other search engines, but focusing on the top five will give you the most bang-for-your-buck.

- **Google**: google.com
- **Yahoo!**: yahoo.com

- **MSN**: msn.com
- **AOL**: aol.com
- **Ask Jeeves**: ask.com

Visit each search engine and read about its policy and procedures on how to submit your site. If you have links pointing to your site, there is a good chance your site has already been crawled and indexed. Before submitting your site, search for your domain name to see whether your site is already listed. You can do this by typing in your URL.

Directories

A directory is also like a search engine, but the indexing of sites is usually done by humans instead of software. When submitting to a directory, you will be required to identify the appropriate category that your site should be listed under. Directories are kind of like yellow pages. Everything is categorized by the type of business. Consumers who use directories like the fact that they can browse a list of websites under the same category.

One of the leading directories is the Open Directory Project (dmoz.org). This particular directory is important because some search engines will actually use your listing in this directory to spider your site. Some search engines will also give you a higher ranking if your site is listed with the Open Directory Project.

So don't forget to list your site with the directories even if you have never heard of them:

- **Open Directory Project**: dmoz.org
- **Yahoo!**: yahoo.com

Search Engine Optimization

Registering your website at the major search engines is relatively simple. The challenge is making your site appear at the top of the search results list when a shopper searches for an eTailer that sells your products or services. To accomplish this feat, you have to optimize your site for the major search engines.

Optimization is more art than science because each search engine uses different search rules. But there are some key things you can do to ensure that your web store does not come up as site number 1,000 in a search results list. Now, there are many books and online services that claim to guarantee top placement in the major search engines if you use their tricks and services. But the search engines regularly change the ways they search the Web, so many of these tricks do not hold true for long.

If you really want to learn the current tricks of the search engine trade, visit Search Engine Watch at searchenginewatch.com. Also, SEOChat at www.seochat.com and webmasterworld at www.webmasterwolrd.com are two other active discussion boards full of invaluable insight into getting better rankings.

Whatever your choice, you need to know the general basics of how search engines search the Web. Each one has a different formula on how it ranks and how you get included into its database. Google, for example, will spider your site for free, whereas others will require a submission fee. The ranking and business inclusion model is always changing. Therefore, you will need to visit each search engine or directory to see how you get your site listed.

> **tip** **Are You Listed in the Search Engines?**
>
> Some search engines will confirm whether your website is already in their database. Here's a way to find out whether your website is listed in the major search engines. Take a look at the URL-checking information along with many other useful tools at Search Engine Watch: http://searchenginewatch.com/ webmasters/article.php/2167861.

So what are some of the main things search engines are looking for when cataloging your website?

- **Meta keywords**: Do you have keywords in your meta tags?
- **Content**: Is your web copy keyword rich? Do your meta keywords appear in the web copy?
- **Link popularity**: How many websites are linking to your site? Is the other site relevant to your keywords? Are there keywords in the text link provided by the other website?
- **Page title**: Does your keyword appear in the page title?

Let's take a look at them now.

It's very important that you take care when creating the page title, page description, page keywords, and the first paragraph of your web pages. The search engines in one way or another will read this text and use it to return a list of search results to web surfers.

Don't make the mistake of creating a page title that's good for people but bad for the search engines. Don't use a title for your page such as "mySoftware

Store—We Sell Computer Software." With a title like that, you're asking to be overlooked by the search engines. Create a unique title for each page. Select a handful of keywords that describe your web page and create a title tag that uses them with the most important words first. Placing your keywords in the beginning of the title will also help if the search engine result truncates your title.

A good title tag for your page would read

> <TITLE>Productivity software for business and home office use—selling word processing, spreadsheet, database, and presentation software including utilities and accessories—mySoftware Store, your store for business productivity</TITLE>

Notice that your company name is near the end of the title tag. Why? Your page description will probably be truncated by the search engine, so you want your most important information on what you offer up front.

Another reason for all this verbiage is that the three most important places to have *keywords* and *key word phrases* are your title tag, your meta tags, and your first paragraph. You want them to all contain the same important words because this will improve your ranking in a search result. Why? Because having all these keywords in all your tags increases your keyword density and improves your rankings.

Identify Keywords

In Chapter 2, "Picking a Customer Niche," we discussed how to research and identify keywords or keyword phrases that consumers will use to search for your product or services. This is the most important step in optimizing your site. Your research will reveal keywords and keyword phrases you never new consumers used to find websites like yours. For example, if I type in the phrase "baby toys" in Overture's keyword selector tool, I get a listing of 100 other keyword phrase variations and how many searches were performed using each phrase during the last month. The phrase "baby toys" returned results such as "toy and baby", "baby Einstein toy", "baby learning toy", "toy baby doll", "baby bath doll", and more. Take a look at the results and identify which keyword phrases apply to your business. Only use the ones you think are relevant and then rank them by number of searches. This will help you prioritize which keywords to target. A site may spend all its time on optimizing for "baby toys" but convert a very low percent of traffic to buyers if the site specializes in a narrow range of products that appeal only to a small subset of the visitors searching for "baby toys." The less popular keyword phrases are less expensive and can create the highest ROI. Remember, even though some keywords may not be as popular, a combination of these low-volume keywords can produce more traffic than some of the more popular keywords. The research will help you target other related keywords and keyword phrases that may not be as competitive.

Misspellings, plurals and synonyms are also good keywords to target.

tip **Using Keyword Phrases**

Consider optimizing your site for keyword phrases (groups of keywords). Keyword phrases are usually less competitive, have a higher conversion rate, and cost less when using pay-per-click advertising services.

Also, don't forget to check out your competition. Take a look at their source code and see whether any of their keywords pertain to your business. Take advantage of their research. To do this, simply go to your competitor's web page, and select View, then slide down to Source and, there they are: These are the keywords and keyword phrases that your competition thinks best describe its business.

The Importance of Meta Tags

Now, let's take a closer look at meta tags.

The meta tags are important to getting a good ranking in the search results. Meta tags come in two flavors— description meta tags and keyword meta tags. The description meta tag is a brief description (about 100–200 characters) of what's on a web page.

The description meta tag looks something like this:

```
<META name="description" content="Productivity software for business
and home office use—selling word processing, spreadsheet, database, and
presentation software including utilities and accessories">
```

The other meta tag is the keyword tag. Create a set of keyword phrases that explain your page or site and list them in the meta tag separated by commas.

After you have your keywords, turn them into key phrases. Be careful about repeating a key phrase. This sends up a red flag for the search engines. Repeating the same keyword more than five times raises another red flag. Do these and many of the search engines will penalize you and hurt you in the search rankings, or not list that page at all.

Here's an example of a keyword meta tag:

<META name="keywords" content="productivity software, word processing, accounting software, spreadsheet software, productivity tools for business, home office computer software, virus protection, modems, surge suppressors">

Finally, pay attention to the first paragraph of the web page you are registering with the search engines. The first paragraph of your web page should duplicate and expand upon everything in your title and meta tags. Make sure the first paragraph has all your key phrases in it. Turn those keywords, key phrases, and title into a welcoming message that will make a good first impression on the consumer visiting your site. Remember you only get one chance to make a first impression with today's web shoppers.

Search experts also point out that keywords/phrases may get better weight when they appear in headings and bold type such as an H1 or H2. Also, the keywords need to be in the ALT tags, internal hyperlinks, anchors, and even in the names of the GIFs and JPEGs.

Adding Meta Tags in Store Editor

So what do you do once you've identified those keywords or keyword phrases? Once you finalize your keyword list, you will need to add them to your meta tags.

Adding Meta Keywords in Store Editor

To add meta keywords, all you need to do is enter the keywords. The Store Editor will automatically generate the META tag automatically. You do not have to enter any HTML. You can add global meta tags or individual meta tags unique to each page for better search engine placement. You can first start with adding global meta tags until you have time to generate individual meta tags.

Adding global meta keywords to all your pages

1. In Store Manager, click on Store Editor.

2. In Store Editor, click on the Variables button in the toolbar.

3. Scroll down to the page properties section. There will be a keyword form box, as seen in Figure 12.1.

4. Enter your keywords or keyword phrases separated by commas.

5. Once you have finished, click on the Update button. Remember you will need to publish your changes.

FIGURE 12.1

Yahoo! Store provides a keyword form box to enter your meta keywords.

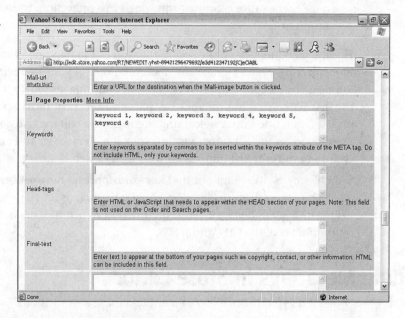

In order to add keywords to individual pages, you will need to override the keyword variable setting:

1. In Store Manager, click on Store Editor.

2. Go to the page you wish to add keywords to and click the Edit button.

3. Click on the Override Variables button.

4. Select the Keyword variable in the drop-down menu to override and click Update, as seen in Figure 12.2.

5. This will return you to the Store Editor edit page. The Keyword variable will appear under the Custom Properties section. You may need to click on the plus button if you do not see the keyword variable. Enter your custom keywords into the keyword form box and click Update.

Adding Meta Description in Store Editor

With meta descriptions, you also have a choice of either adding global or individual meta descriptions. Unlike meta keywords, you will need to add some simple HTML. Store Editor does not automatically generate the HTML for you.

FIGURE 12.2

There are many
variables that
can be overrid-
den. The avail-
able variables
are displayed in
the drop-down
menu.

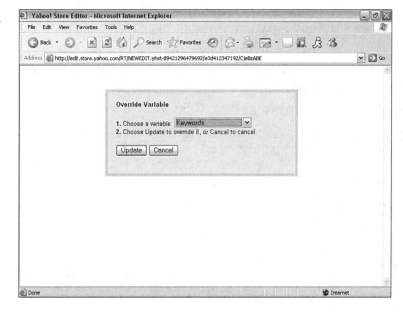

Adding global meta description to all your pages

1. In Store Manager, click on Store Editor.

2. In Store Editor, click on the red arrow to display the Advanced toolbar.

3. Click on the Variables button.

4. Scroll down to the Page Properties section until you see the Head-tags variable. Copy and paste the following meta description tag and replace the description with your own description, as seen in Figure 12.3.

   <meta name="description" content="**Insert your own description here.**">

5. Click Update once you are done and publish your changes.

Adding unique meta description to individual pages

1. In Store Manager, click on Store Editor.

2. Go to the page you wish to add a unique meta description to and click the Edit button.

3. Click on the Override Variable button.

4. Select the Head-tags variable in the drop-down menu to override and click Update.

5. This will return you to the Store Editor edit page. The Head-tags variable will appear under the Custom Properties section.

6. Scroll down to the Custom Properties section until you see the Head-tags variable. Copy and paste the following meta description tag and replace the description with your own description:

   <meta name="description" content="**Insert your own description here.**">

7. Once you are done, click Update and publish your changes.

FIGURE 12.3

Yahoo! Store does not provide a form box to enter your meta description like it does for meta keywords. You will need to add your own meta description HTML as shown.

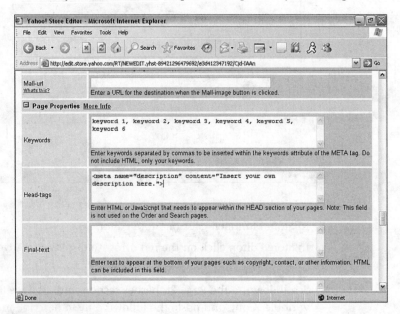

Keyword-Related Content

Search engines are very smart. They will even index every single word on your web page. It is extremely important to use your targeted keywords or keyword phrases throughout the content of your web page. Large sites have an advantage because they have a lot of content with lots of keywords. When writing copy for your websites, remember to include your targeted keywords.

Before you start writing your web copy, have your keyword list handy. This will help ensure that you include the keywords in your copy.

Although meta keywords and descriptions are important, rich keyword content is more important. You will need fresh, unique, and lengthy (about 450 words) content for each page you want high ranking. If you are using content from manufacturers or other websites, make sure you add, reword, and change the original content. This will prevent your site from getting penalized by the search engines' duplicate content filters.

Here are some ideas to help you generate relevant and unique content:

- Write reviews about your products.
- Allow customers to add reviews about the products.
- Include testimonials from customers.
- Add a frequently updated blog.
- Revise product descriptions from manufacturers.
- Create a monthly newsletter.
- Write industry related articles.
- Ask other to contribute to your site.

tip Don't try to squeeze every single keyword or keyword phrase into every single page. Group them along with your meta keywords and meta description.

Link Popularity

Search engines also rank your site by the number and quality of links pointing to your site from outside websites. Your ranking will also improve if your targeted keywords are part of the text link pointing to your site.

For example, instead of using your company name as your text link, use keywords such as "discount books and computers" as your text link.

caution Although tempting, don't add your site to link farms. Link farms are web pages created solely for linking to other sites. They contain no content and are only used to "prove" to search engines that you have a popular site that many others link to. These link farms will almost certainly get you banned from search engines.

So how do you get others to link to your site? The best way to get links is to have a lot of valuable information. Like the saying goes, "Content is king." If you have good content, other websites will add your site as a resource. Another way to get links to your website is through link exchanges, contacting and partnering with other websites. They add your link to their website and you add their link to your website.

Page Title

Search engines also look at your page title for keywords when indexing your page. Do not start your page title with your company name unless consumers are using your company name as a search phrase. Use keywords first and move the company name toward the end of the title if it needs to be included. Create a compelling page title to include your most important keywords. Search engines such as Google will actually display your page title as the link. If it's not compelling, the consumer will not click on the link even though you get top ranking. It would be a shame if you did all that work, got your page up into the top three results, and had your customers click on your competitors just because your title didn't have a compelling call to action.

Here's how you create the page title in Store Editor.

The Name variable or field is used to create your page title. Whatever you input in the Name field will be displayed as your page title. You can go back and edit the page title anytime.

1. In Store Manager, click on the Store Editor link.

2. Navigate to the page you would like to change the title and click the Edit button.

3. Type in the new page title and click the Update button. Once you have finished, publish your changes (see figure 12.4).

FIGURE 12.4

The page title is located in the Name field box in Store Editor.

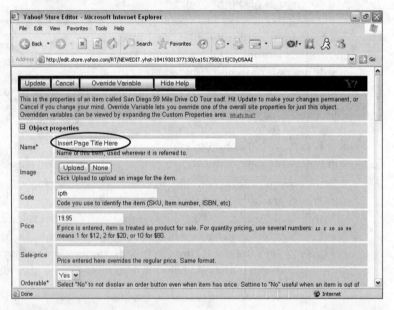

Search Engine Strategy

One of the major issues most website owners face when trying to optimize their site is that they don't have goals. No game plan. They just don't know where to start. The following is a list of goals used by some of the leading successful search engine optimizers.

- Establish at least 25 external links back to your website from reputable sites. Try to include keywords in those incoming text links.
- Submit your site to vortals (vertical portals) and directories.
- Rearrange your keyword phrases and mix and match words.
- Make sure the meta keywords match keywords in your content page. Avoid adding keywords in your meta tags that aren't available on your page.
- Create page titles with your keywords.
- Add keywords in your meta description.
- Content on your web page should contain at least 300–450 words, including your keywords or keyword phrases.
- Include at least 8 keyword hyperlinks (and anchors).
- Have at least 8 keyword alt tags.
- Add keywords in your comments code. Even though the comments code does not show up on your web page, search engines read it.
- Create page and graphic file names to include your keywords.

Although it's never guaranteed that you will get top ranking with this or any other strategy, this will at least help get you started.

Software

Optimizing your site can be a daunting and time-consuming task. There is software available to help automate some of the process such as analyzing keyword density, generating keyword position reports, submitting your URL to search engines quickly, generating link popularity reports, and more. Using these tools can help you save time and money. You may download free trial versions of the following software via their websites.

- **Web Position Gold**: webpositiongold.com
- **Internet Business Promoter (IBP)**: axandra.com
- **Go Rank**: gorank.com

Resources

So how do you keep up with all the industry changes and new search optimization methods? If you are the do-it-yourself type, here's a list of resources.

- **Search Engine Watch (searchenginewatch.com)**: Great articles and updates from leading industry experts.

- **Search Engine News (searchenginenews.com)**: They offer a monthly updated eBook titled *The Unfair Advantage Book on Winning the Search Engine Wars* with every subscription.

- **Search Engine Strategies Conference and Expo (searchenginestrategies.com)**: Monthly conference discussing top issues and marketing strategies. Learn strategies from top experts. Check the website for conferences in your area.

- **MyEcommerceSuccess (MyEcommerceSuccess.com)**: For a list of qualified search optimization companies.

Using Yahoo! Store Search Stats

So how do you know if visitors to your site are coming from search engines? You can view how many visitors, which search engine they came from, and what keywords they used to find your site by viewing the web stats.

To view stats

1. In Store Manager, click on the References link under the Statistics column.

2. Scroll down until you see the list of referring URLs. You can click on the Details link (see Figure 12.5) next to each referring URL from search engines to view details on query terms used to locate your site.

Now you have a search engine optimization (SEO) strategy and enough information to get you started and keep you busy for quite some time. For more advanced search engine marketing techniques, take a look at the companion book *Succeeding At Your Yahoo! Store*.

Now you're almost ready to open your doors and take orders. But before you do that, you need to understand how to manage the day-to-day business of running a Yahoo! Store. We will discuss that in the next chapter.

FIGURE 12.5

You can view details of query terms for each search engine by clicking on the details link.

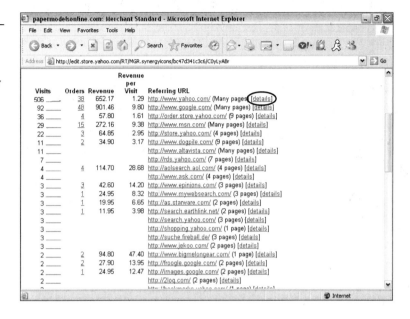

Marketing and Merchandising Your Store Using Yahoo! Tools

In Chapter 10, we discussed how to bring visitors to your newly established online storefront, and for little or no money. Now it's time to look at the different marketing and merchandising tools available to you through Yahoo! store. These are not free, but do offer an affordable way to merchandise your eCommerce store and drive shoppers to your website.

Yahoo! store offers ways to develop your merchandising strategy, create a direct marketing program, and receive what are called Yahoo! merchant reviews to help attract customers to your Yahoo! store.

Let's first look at developing a merchandising strategy and how Yahoo! store can help.

Developing Your Merchandising Strategy

Merchandising is the strategy of promoting goods inside a store, or in the case of a Yahoo! store, on an online storefront. In the real world, retailers promote in-store sales in a number of ways, using product positioning inside the store, carefully selecting where products are positioned on store shelves, setting up point of purchase displays to spur add-on sales, and even having timely promotional events.

Case in point: Ever wonder why products such as milk and eggs are at the back of a grocery store? These items are purchased frequently and thus drive us to the grocery store on a consistent basis. The grocery store knows this and makes us walk through rows of items throughout the store that we might not have considered buying if the store hadn't brought them to our attention for possible purchase. This is one form of merchandising.

In general, merchandising is how and where you position and display your products or service in your online storefront, including extras such as timely promotions and limited-time sales events. These merchandising tactics will have an impact on your sales. Other merchandising tactics include making it easy for shoppers to find what they are looking for and offering complimentary products or services related to what they are buying.

Your home page is a very important element of your merchandising strategy. It goes without saying that your home page receives the greatest amount of traffic on your eCommerce site. This is valuable real estate and should be exploited for merchandising purposes. Think of your home page as a place to showcase your most popular products, limited time specials, or seasonal events, and a way to draw shoppers into your store.

Automate Your Merchandising

Frequent rotation of well-priced products or services on your home page will encourage shoppers to return again and again to your storefront to see what is new.

Yahoo! can help you in this regard. Yahoo! provides several tools in Merchant Standard and Merchant Professional that automate key merchandising functions such as cross-selling, discount offers, and gift certificates. These tools are all available in the Store Manager.

Product Merchandising Page Templates

In the Store Tag Hub, you will find several page layouts that you can cut and paste into a web design application, such as SiteBuilder, to help you quickly create product merchandising pages. Layouts are available for product detail pages and category pages. These layouts are completely customizable, so you can create the exact look that you would like for your site. To add your products to these layouts, you just need to add the appropriate Store Tag codes.

Yahoo! offers three *free* merchandising tools (depending on the Merchant Solution package you choose) to help you promote the sales of your products or service (see Figure 13.1). They are

- A cross-sell engine
- Gift certificates
- Coupons

FIGURE 13.1

Using one or all three of the free merchandising tools (cross-sell engine, gift certificates, and coupons) will help generate sales. These tools are available in the Store Manager.

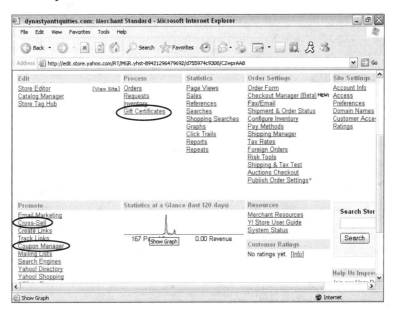

Cross-Sell Engine

Cross-selling is an excellent way to increase sales from an existing purchase. In short, cross-selling is the tactic of offering additional products to current purchasers in an attempt to increase customer spending per visit. In other words, it's the ability to identify customers who have purchased a specific product or service in order to sell them similar or related products or services. Cross-selling works because customers are most inclined to buy at checkout time.

Yahoo! offers a cross-selling engine for your Yahoo! store. This is a very valuable merchandising tool. With it, you can create cross-selling opportunities using up to 100 related products in your store. You can create special offers and discounts using the cross-selling engine to entice shoppers to buy other products from your store.

Cross-selling is an excellent strategy for boosting a customer's spending per visit. Yahoo!'s cross-selling engine will automatically suggest related products to purchase when customers place items into their shopping carts.

For example, if a person places a digital camera in his shopping cart, the cross-selling engine can automatically recommend a memory card, batteries, or a photo-editing software application. You can determine which products are recommended, set start and end dates for special cross-sell offers or seasonal promotions, and even provide special pricing for cross-sell items to encourage your users to buy right away. The cross-sell engine is only available in Merchant Standard and Merchant Professional.

Gift Certificates

Why not print your own private-labeled currency? That's what gift certificates are because they can be spent only at your store. Gift certificates can be offered directly from your Yahoo! store. Yahoo! offers the use of gift certificates with its Merchant Standard and Professional plans.

Customers can buy and send electronic gift certificates from your site and the recipient can redeem the gift certificate during the checkout process. In addition, the gift certificate service will let you track the number of gift certificates you have issued and which have not been redeemed from the Store Manager.

FIGURE 13.2

Gift certificates are a great way to boost sales. The Gift Certificate code is usually emailed to the customer, but you may also send a printed certificate. The certificate code will need to be included on the paper certificate.

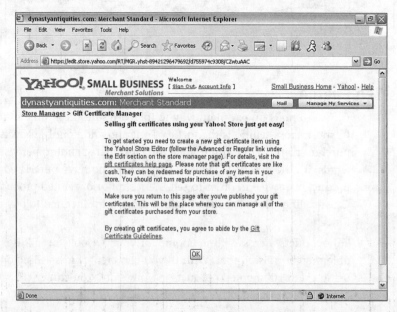

Coupons

Offering discount coupons is another merchandising strategy to attract shoppers to your web store and increase sales. At first you might think of coupons as used only in the real world. And, yes, you can offer coupons on your site that can be printed off and used in your real-world store. But if you're a pure eCommerce company, why not offer them directly on your site? Here's how.

With the Coupon Manager feature available in the Merchant Standard and Merchant professional store packages, you can create coupons that shoppers can redeem at your store. These coupons can be created for any purpose, such as a particular percentage or dollar amount off or free shipping. You can promote these coupons in your advertising, email, and marketing materials as a customer acquisition or retention strategy. Customers can redeem these coupons at checkout. The dollar amount or discount you specified will automatically be calculated and displayed on the following page. You can also track the performance of specific coupons, so you can see how many times they've been used, check how much revenue they've generated, and review graphs of their performance over time.

FIGURE 13.3

With Coupon Manager, you can also set a minimum purchase amount and expiration date. Coupons are a great way to generate repeat customers.

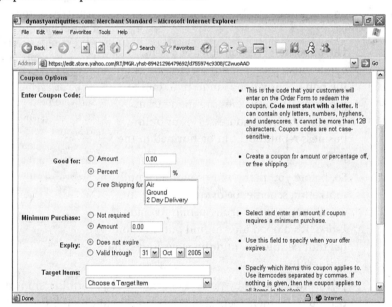

Permission Marketing—Direct Marketing

One of the most cost-effective ways to promote and market your web store is through direct email. There simply isn't an easier, cheaper, more direct way to talk to someone online. There are other benefits to creating and managing a

proprietary mailing list, such as maintaining relationships with current customers, increasing repeat customers to your storefront, and promoting your
brand in the marketplace. And keeping your business and the products or
services it sells in front of your customers and prospects is one of the best ways
to reach your target audience to achieve your goals.

Free Info Download the free informative article titled "Reach Out & Touch Someone—6 Ways to Grow
Your House List for Fun & Profit" at www.MyEcommerceSuccess.com.

Though it sounds easy, email marketing
does take work to do right. You must start
with a clean email list of people who
have confirmed their willingness to
receive your email offer (have opted-in),
then target and personalize that offer for
the best response. And that's the most
important part of email marketing—send
only to those who have asked to receive
your offers.

The opposite of responsible, or opt-in,
email marketing is spam. And spam is
the bane of any good email marketing
program. Though sales are made from
spamming email addresses, your online
business reputation can be harmed in the
process.

So, before you plan your grandiose email
marketing scheme, be aware that opt-in
email marketing is really *permission marketing*. It's a good idea to find out how to
get that permission and the ways to get the
best results.

caution

What's Opt-in Email?

Opt-in email is the direct opposite
of spam. People who opt-in to an
email list have said in advance that
they are willing to receive unsolicited email from companies on
the Net that meet the list criteria.
For example, someone who would
like to be kept informed of newly
released software might opt-in to
an email list that announces new
software products. Under no circumstances should you use bulk
lists, often sold on CD-ROMs. They
typically contain names of people
who have not agreed to receive
unsolicited email. Be aware that if
your ISP receives complaints about
your company's emailing practices,
it could shut down your account.

Just what is meant by permission marketing? Permission marketing means
getting consumers' permission to email them an offer *before* it shows up in the
email box.

It works like this. When a consumer visits a permission marketing–enabled
eBusiness, registers at it, or buys something from it, the consumer is asked,
"Would you like to receive information from us periodically about new sales

or receive our newsletter?" The consumer then responds with either a yes or no by clicking a box. If the answer is yes, then the consumer has given permission. If it's no, he hasn't.

An important point to remember is how you construct your email offer.

First of all, sell benefits, not features of your product or service. For example, suppose you're selling diet food. Instead of stating "Our food contains low fat or low calories," say in your offer, "Lose 10 pounds in 30 days!" Selling benefits rather than features gives your recipients something they can identify with. Also, make your offer sound exclusive and for a limited time. This makes the recipient feel special and motivated to take action immediately.

Getting permission is extremely important for your email marketing strategy and the reputation of your eBusiness. So plan to do it right. One good way is to use the services of Yahoo! store.

Creating and Using Permission-Based Mailing Lists

There are several ways to build a permission email list:

- Offer a reason for a visitor to give you her email address, such as a free subscription to your newsletter, a free download of a media or text file, or free entry to a contest or sweepstakes.

- If you have a business in the real world, ask customers for their email addresses.

- Include your email subscription information on all of your offline materials, including print advertising and direct mail.

You can even use your Yahoo! store to collect email addresses at the point of purchase. When customers make purchases at your Yahoo! store, they have the option to enter an email address where they'll receive correspondence related to their orders and special offers from your company. Yahoo! Merchant Solutions automatically maintains this as a secure emailing list for your store, which you can later use to send out direct email marketing programs or your own email newsletter.

Free Info Download the free informative article entitled "Reach out and Touch Someone: 6 Ways to Grow Your House List" at www.MyEcommerceSuccess.com.

If you would like to increase your direct marketing campaign beyond the emails you collect from each order, Yahoo! offers two fee-based programs, Campaigner by GOT and infoUSA.

GOT Campaigner

Campaigner can help you grow your customer base, increase sales, create repeat customers, and measure the ROI (return on investment) of each direct emailing campaign (see Figure 13.4). The cost through Yahoo! is as little as $25 a month and you can grow your permission-based contact list as easily as adding a Subscribe Now button on any page of your online storefront.

FIGURE 13.4

GOT Campaigner's easy-to-use wizards will guide you step-by-step through the process of creating an email campaign.

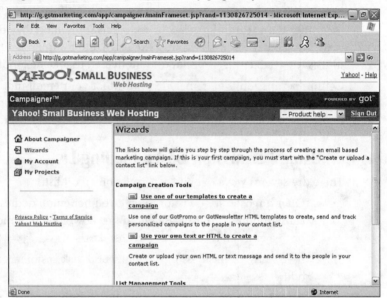

Though GOT does not provide any email lists, its Campaigner can help grow your business using web-based email marketing tools. You can upload your own list or enter one online; it manages bounce backs and unsubscribes automatically, and stores lists of any size in a secure account.

Campaigner's web-based templates let you insert a variety of graphics into an email message, such as logos and pictures in color. No technical knowledge is required. And you can schedule and send your direct emails out whenever you like. With Campaigner, you can publish electronic newsletters, run promotions, send out announcements, distribute online catalogs, and manage a permission-based prospect and customer list.

InfoUSA Prospecting Lists

Renting opt-in lists is a great way to promote your business and build a customer base. To provide business and consumer mailing lists and sales leads to Yahoo! store owners, Yahoo! has partnered with infoUSA (see Figure 13.5). For as little as 10 cents per name, you can rent a mailing list from infoUSA.

FIGURE 13.5

infoUSA has
hundreds of
email lists to
choose from.
You can search
through their
lists to find your
targeted market.

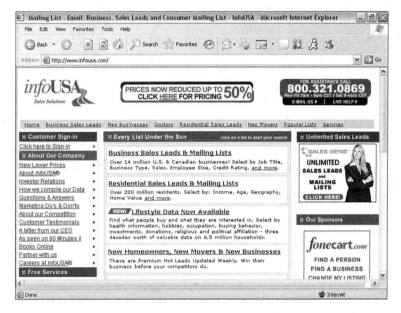

How can this help market your businesses? Acquiring new customers is a
never-ending job for a business. No matter what you sell, you need a constant
flow of new customers to keep your business growing. You can use the tools
provided by infoUSA to analyze who your customers are and use this information to find new prospects just like them. infoUSA will provide you with qualified leads any way you want them—via email or download, or delivered on
disk, labels, or sales leads cards.

Register with Online Shopping Destinations

One of the best places to find potential customers for your online business is
at the shopping destination web sites. Yahoo! Small Business customers can
take advantage of exclusive discounts on marketing services from Yahoo! and
other leading vendors.

Start by submitting your website to Yahoo! Product Submit. Your products will
be prominently featured in Yahoo! Shopping at shopping.yahoo.com as seen
in Figure 13.6, giving you access to millions of online shoppers. It will also be
included in the Yahoo! Product Search and Buyers Guide Pages. Your products
are included on a cost-per-click fee based on the product category you choose.
You only pay when a lead is generated to your website. Yahoo! offers discounts
to store owners and you will receive 20% off of the fee per click. Identifying
what keywords customers are using to find products like yours will help you
refine your product titles and descriptions to achieve better ranking.

To sign up for Product Submit

1. From the Manage My Services control panel, click on Store Manager.

2. In Store Manager, click on Yahoo! Shopping under the Promote column.

3. From the Product Submit page, complete the account setup questionnaire pages.

> **tip** Using Product Submit is a great way to quickly test a new product. You can view statistics to determine the ROI (Rate of Return) of a product by the number of visitors to that particular product compared to the number of buyers.

FIGURE 13.6

Yahoo! Product Submit will give you access to millions of online shoppers. The product search is located directly on Yahoo!'s homepage or you can visit shopping.yahoo.com.

Next, register with Google's product search engine Froogle. Customers can search for products on Google's home page or visit froogle.com as seen in Figure 13.7. Froogle is completely free and there is no cost per click advertising. Yes, I said FREE! Google receives millions of visitors each day and the Froogle product search is available right on Google's home page.

You can also control the product information by uploading a product feed. A product feed is a spreadsheet or text file containing your product information that you upload to the Froogle's system. Froogle uses this information to properly display your product information. You can download a sample product feed and instructions from the Froogle website.

To sign up for Froogle

1. Go to Froogle.com.

2. Click on the Information for Merchants link at the bottom of the page.

3. Click on the Get Started button on the right side of the page. This will take you to another page where you can create an account.

FIGURE 13.7

Millions of people visit Google each day and the Froogle product search is right on Google's homepage. There is absolutely no cost to list your product in Froogle.

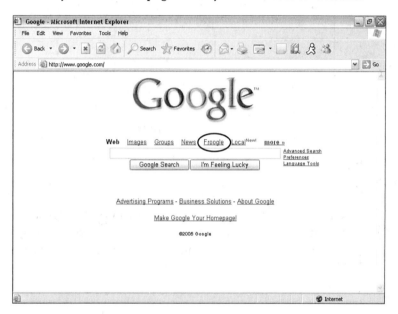

Yahoo! Merchant Ratings and Reviews

Yahoo! merchant ratings and reviews are feedback from your customers, as seen in Figure 13.8. The rating system is based on a 1–5 star scale. You have the option of turning Customer Ratings on so that your customers can have an opportunity to rate your product and services. Customers are given a set of questions to answer and they also have an opportunity to write their own comments. Enabling Customer Ratings will not only help you receive valuable feedback about your service and product, but will allow your potential customer to see third-party comments about your product and services.

In order to participate in Yahoo! Shopping, customer ratings must be enabled. Customers who visit Yahoo! Shopping will see your star rating next to your products.

> **tip** In order to receive high ratings, make sure your products are well packaged, always return phone calls and emails in a timely manner, and over-deliver the promised shipping deliver date. Calling customers you have provided excellence service to and asking them to rate your product will also help improve ratings.

FIGURE 13.8

Merchant ratings provide a quick glance view of your company based on a 1 to 5 star scale.

Now that you're equipped with the basic tools for promoting your Yahoo! store, it's time to turn on attention to the day-to-day management of your business. The next chapter will focus on managing your work flow.

Part V

Managing Day-to-Day Business

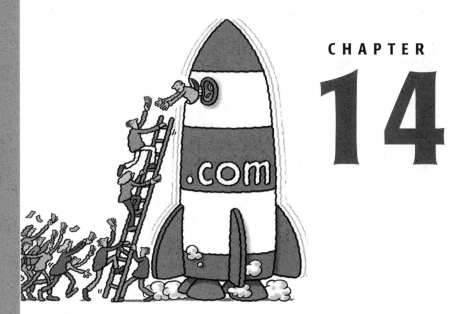

To Do List— Managing Workflow

Now that your site is up and running and the orders are starting to pour in, you will need to manage your work-flow in order to keep your operation running smoothly. Develop a checklist or a step-by-step list of duties. You can develop a list for daily operations or you can create multiple lists for specific tasks.

Here's a sample checklist of an order process:

1. Check email for new orders.
2. Review order for accuracy and fraud.
3. Confirm order with customer (optional).
4. Process credit card.
5. Package order.
6. Go to mail center or schedule for pickup.
7. Update inventory list.

If you are working with others, assign a name to each task.

Processing Orders

Processing orders can be one of the more enjoyable duties of an online business. After all, this is the part of the business where you begin the process of receiving money in your bank account.

Receiving Orders via Email or Fax

Merchant Solutions allows you to receive new order confirmation via email, fax, or both (fax only available with Standard and Professional packages). You can even set it to send notifications to multiple email addresses or fax numbers. This is convenient if you have more than one person who needs to be informed of the new order.

Once you receive the order, you will want to review and process the credit card before shipping the product. Although the credit card was approved and you have an approval code, the transaction can still be declined when you try to process the credit card. For example, from the time the order was placed and the time you attempt to process the credit card, the card may be cancelled, go over its limit, or even expire.

To process orders

1. In Store Manager, click on the Orders link under the Process column.

2. If you haven't already entered your security key, a login window will appear. Enter your security key in the form box. This will take you to the Order Manager.

3. Locate the order you would like to process. If you have new orders pending, the first new order number will appear in the specific order box (see Figure 14.1). Click the View button. This will take you to that specific order.

4. Before you process the order, you will want to review it. If the order looks okay, scroll down until you see the Sale button (see Figure 14.2). Click on the Sale button. Another window will appear confirming whether it was processed properly or whether the process failed.

5. Click the OK button. This will take you back to the order. If you have other orders that need to be processed, click on the Next button above the order information. This will take you to the next order.

Note: Clicking on the Sale button adds your transaction to a batch along with all other orders that you processed. This will also include refunds and credits, if any. Once a day between 6 and 11 p.m. (PST), your batch of transactions is processed automatically by Yahoo! Merchant Solutions. You can also submit the batch immediately if you click on the Submit Batch link in the Manual Transaction Control Panel.

FIGURE 14.1

The first order number from the series of new orders will appear in the specific order form box. Click the View button to start processing the first new order.

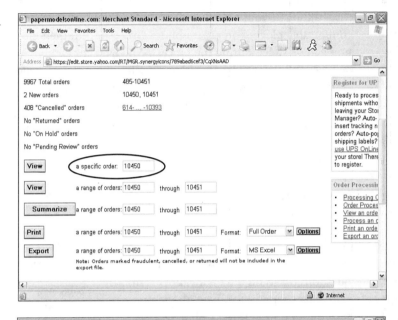

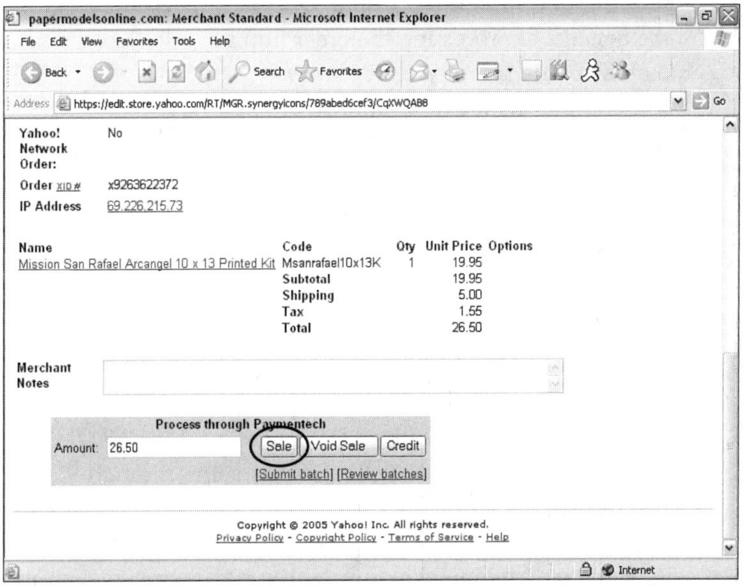

FIGURE 14.2

To process orders, click on the Sale button. The Sale button is located at the bottom of each order.

Taking Orders over the Phone

Not all orders will originate via your website. Depending on how your business is set up, you may receive orders via fax, in person, by mail, or by phone. Also, although your website order form is secure, some customers will not feel comfortable placing an order online. They fear that their credit card information will be stolen during the process. And who can blame them? Once in awhile you'll hear news of hackers stealing thousand of credit card numbers from websites and even large banks. The hacker may or may not do anything with the stolen credit card information, but the fear is still there.

When taking an order via the phone, you will need to obtain all the necessary information from the customers to process the order later, or you can go through the order process online while the customer is on the phone. If you decide not to process the order online immediately, it is recommended that you create a form to gather the information from the customer. If you are planning on creating a form, you should go through the order process and write down all the questions asked on the online order form. This will ensure that you get all the necessary information for processing. One of the benefits of processing the order immediately online is that you will know whether the credit card is approved. This will not only reduce fraud, but will prevent you from having to call the customer back if the card was declined for some reason.

caution It is strongly recommended that merchants place orders online in their store while the customer is on the phone. Recording credit card info on paper or a spreadsheet (neither of which are secure methods) is a violation of CISP/PCI security protocols, which govern how, when, and where credit card info can be stored by merchants. This could result in large fines from card associations, or merchants could lose their merchant account if this information is stolen.

Processing Manual Orders

Once you receive an order offline, you will need to manually process the credit card. There are two ways to do this: You can use the Manual Transaction Manager or you can go through the order process as if you were the customer placing an order online. The benefit of going through the process is that you will be able to capture all the customer and product data for reporting purposes in the future. Using the Manual Transaction Manager as seen in Figure 14.3 will only require you to enter the card number, expiration date, amount, CVS, and billing address. There is no place to input product information, shipping address, and customer information such as name, phone number, and email address.

Although it is a little bit more work to go through the order process for the customer and fill out all the information, this will allow you to capture the necessary data for future use.

To process manual orders

1. In Store Manager, click on the Manual Transactions link under the Process column.

2. Fill-out the required information as seen in Figure 14.3 and click on the Sale button.

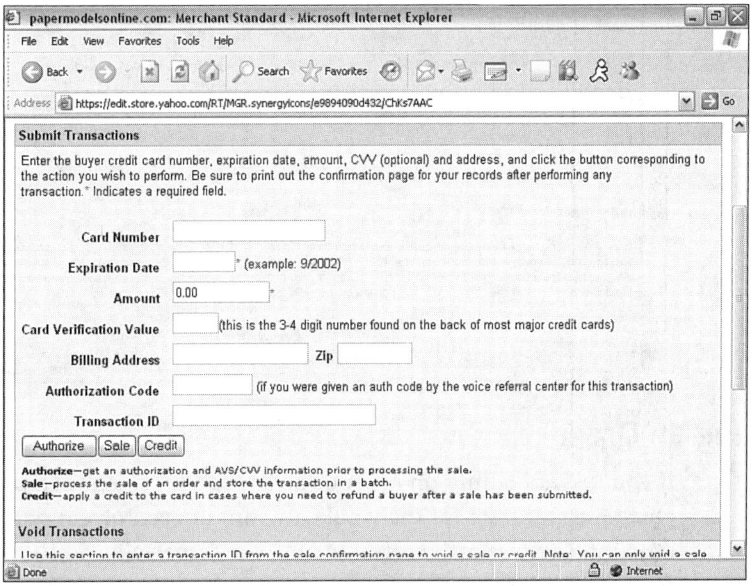

FIGURE 14.3

You can process offline orders by using the Manual Transaction Manager.

Retrieving Orders

To respond to existing customer inquires such as "I ordered x, but you sent me b," "you charged me twice," or "where is my shipment?," you will need to pull up their order information. There are three ways to retrieve an order, as seen in Figure 14.4. You can retrieve the order using the exact order number; view a range of orders to find the order you are searching for; or search for the order using the customer's name, phone number, email address, street address, city, ZIP Code, last four digits of the credit card, or order date.

To retrieve an order

1. In Store Manager, click on the Orders link under the Process column.

2. If you are searching by order number, type the order number in the first field box and then click on the View button. If you are searching by order range, type in the beginning order number and ending order

number in the Range of Orders field box and then click on the View button. If you are searching by keyword, scroll down to the Order Lookup search box, type in the keyword, and click the Search button.

FIGURE 14.4

You can retrieve orders by keyword search, order number, or range of orders.

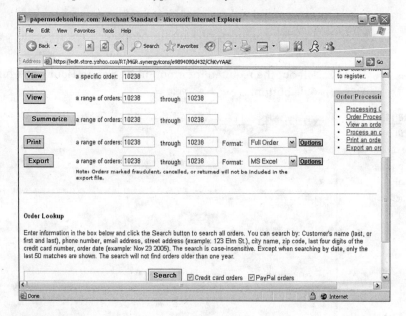

Crediting an Order

If you need to refund an order or give credit for a returned product, you can credit the customer for the whole amount or even give a partial credit amount. Giving partial credit is common, especially if your return policy does not include the shipping cost or you have a restocking fee for returned product. Let's take a look at how to credit the customer's credit card:

1. In Store Manger, click on the Orders link under the Process column.

2. Search for the order you would like to give credit to.

3. Scroll down to the bottom of the order and type in the amount you would like to credit, and then click on the Credit button (see Figure 14.5).

Voiding an Order

If the order was processed and you clicked on the Sale button, the order can still be voided if it has not been batch submitted. Batches are submitted between 6 and 11 p.m. (PST) unless you manually submitted the batch. If an order has been batch submitted and the credit card has been debited, you will need to issue a credit. Once you void an order, it will not be included in the sales statistics. Voiding orders is common when you receive duplicate orders. Some customers will accidentally click on the Submit order button twice. You might also receive a cancellation request from a customer after the order has been placed. Note: If you receive an error message that no transaction is pending when trying to void an order, that means that the batch was submitted and you will need to issue a credit.

To void an order

1. In Store Manager, click on the Orders link under the Process column.

2. Retrieve the order you would like to void.

3. Scroll down until you see the Void Sale button (see Figure 14.6) next to the Sale button. Click on the Void Sale button.

FIGURE 14.5

You will need to credit an order if the order has already been batch submitted and the credit card of the customer has been debited.

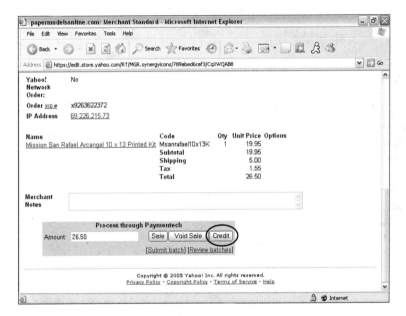

Cancelling an Order

If the order has not been processed and you have not clicked on the Sale button, you can cancel the order by clicking the Cancelled radio button and clicking the Modify button. Like voiding orders, canceling an order will also remove the order from the sales statistics.

To cancel an order

1. In Store Manager, click on the Orders link under the Process column.

2. Retrieve the order you would like to Cancel.

3. Click on the Cancelled radio button (see Figure 14.7) in the Mark Order box and also click on the Modify button above the Mark Order box.

FIGURE 14.6
To void orders, click on the Void Sale button. This will void the order and remove the order from the sales statistics.

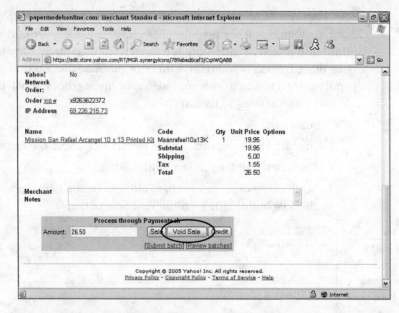

FIGURE 14.7
You may cancel an order if the order has not been processed. Cancelling an order will remove the order from the sales statistics.

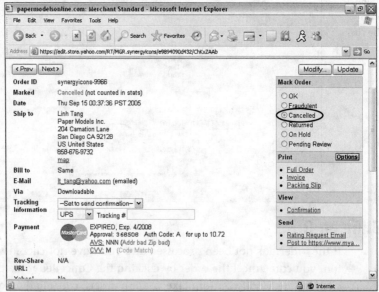

Marking an Order

In addition to marking an order Cancelled to void an order, there are five more options for marking orders: OK, Fraudulent, Returned, On Hold, and Pending Review. The default setting is OK. This is very useful, especially if an order is on hold or pending review. The order number will appear on the home page of the Order Manager, as seen in Figure 14.8. If you receive a lot of orders, this will help you remember that the particular order(s) has not been resolved.

FIGURE 14.8

If an order is marked, the results will appear on the home page of the Order Manager. This will help you remember to review the order.

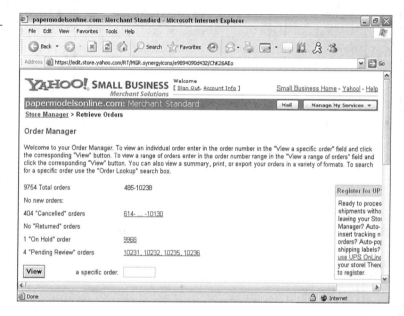

For additional information on ordering processing, download the Merchant Solutions Payment Processing Guide at http://help.yahoo.com/help/us/store/order/order-23.html.

Reviewing Orders for Fraud

Any person experienced in eCommerce knows that building an online business takes a lot of work. Nothing can be worse than seeing all your hard work lost through fraud, especially credit card fraud.

Now you would think that your bank would protect you. Not so. Why doesn't your bank protect you against fraud? Because your merchant agreement says it can't. It's called the MOTO rule.

> **caution**
>
> **MOTO (Mail Order/ Telephone Order) Rule**
>
> Transactions by merchants on the Net fall under the heading of MOTO. Most credit card merchant account agreements leave you, the merchant, 100% liable for fraud committed at your website.

If a credit charge is reversed by request from the card holder, your bank will hit you with a chargeback fee. If you accrue too many chargebacks, your merchant account can be terminated. After one is terminated, it's nearly impossible to get another merchant account.

It's not a pretty prospect when you think about it. And knowing that it's pretty much guaranteed that you will experience an attempt to defraud you sooner or later darkens the picture even further. So to protect yourself, you should review each order for possible fraud before fulfilling it.

So what should you look for when reviewing your order for fraud? Here are a few things to watch for:

- Larger order total than normal
- Shipping address different from the billing address
- Shipping to PO boxes
- Order requesting overnight shipment
- Multiple orders from the same credit card
- Multiple credit cards used by the same IP address
- Credit card does not match the AVS verification
- Multiple orders of the same item
- International orders

Here are some other things to keep in mind:

- Don't assume that merely verifying a credit card—getting an authorization number—is sufficient fraud protection. The verification process checks two things. First, it checks whether the credit card has been reported stolen. Second, it checks whether the credit line has sufficient credit to fund the purchase.
- Your first level of fraud protection is *AVS*. AVS stands for *Address Verification Service*. But it has its limitations. AVS compares the billing address of the customer with the records held by the card issuer. If the card number and billing address match, AVS gives it a thumbs-up. The problem is that the card could still be stolen and a thief can ask that the order be shipped to another address. AVS has other problems too. AVS only works for addresses in the United States. So, if you have an international order, AVS will not help. If you sell software or information that can be downloaded instantly, AVS provides no protection. A thief with a valid billing address that corresponds to a stolen credit card number can cause the AVS system to give an instant approval and your instant buy becomes an instant fraud!

- If you don't use AVS, make sure the customer's billing address matches the shipping address. If it doesn't, ask the buyer why he or she wants the order shipped to another address.

- Ask for TWO phone numbers, work and home. Then do a telephone number search on suspected fraudulent orders.

- Let potential crooks know you check for fraud by notifying them with notices and images on your order forms. This also lets potential customers know that you are serious about fraud and fraudulent orders will turned over to the proper authorities.

- Look at the products being ordered. Does it match similar fraudulent orders you caught in the past? Be careful of big orders such as three MP3 players at once.

- If the customer demands overnight delivery, this too can be a sign of a fraudulent order. Since the scam artist isn't paying for it, he doesn't care how much it costs and he'll want to get it in a hurry.

Look at the email address that is provided. Thieves try to hide their identity by using free email addresses such as the free email services of Hotmail, MSN, or Yahoo!

- Another clue is a suspicious billing address such as 123 Main Street.

- And finally, if someone places a very valuable order and asks that it be left at the front door, be suspicious. A thief may be using that address as a drop-off point. If an order is for a high-priced item, request that it be signed for.

> **tip** Checking Addresses and Phone Numbers for Accuracy
>
> You can check to see whether an address is real by using Yahoo! Maps at maps.yahoo.com. You can also purchase a database of phone numbers on a CD or you can use services such as www.anywho.com or www.switchboard.com, where you can do a reverse search on a phone number. This will allow you to confirm the contact information for the phone number that the customer has provided.

Although your order may meet one or more of these criteria, it does not necessarily mean the order is fraudulent. But if you suspect fraud, follow these steps:

1. Call the customer. Use the phone numbers you requested and collected from him. When you contact him, don't automatically assume that you're dealing with a thief. The customer could have entered incorrect information and you don't want to offend him and lose the sale. In

general though, a thief will not want to have a long conversation with you.

2. If the phone number is wrong, try contacting the customer via email for a valid phone number.

3. If the billing address doesn't match or is incorrect, ask him to give it to you again. If the area code doesn't match the billing address's city, ask why.

4. Ask the customer for the name and phone number of the establishment that issued the card. Both are printed on the back. If the customer cannot supply it, this is a sign that he doesn't physically have the card, just the number.

If you still feel uncomfortable with an order even after talking to the customer, ask him for payment in advance. And if you're hit with a fraudulent order, document all contacts. This will give you greater protection and a better fighting chance of getting your money or product back.

Remember it takes a lot of orders to replace just one order lost to fraud. So, it's better to pass on the ones that you're not 100% certain about. So follow these tips and protect your business. No one else will!

Using Yahoo! Risk Tools to Prevent Future Fraud Orders

So what should you do when the order is an actual fraudulent order? To help prevent additional fraudulent orders from the same person, Merchant Solutions has built-in risk tools such as the IP blocking tool. An IP address is a set of numbers unique to the computer that placed the order. It allows for communication between sender and receiver. You can block a specific IP address or a range of IP addresses. Although this will not guarantee that the same person will not attempt do it again from another computer, it will surely slow him down and hopefully make it not worth the trouble to try it again.

Every order includes the IP address of the computer used to place the order, as seen in Figure 14.9. If the order is fraudulent, take the IP address displayed in the order and add it to the list of blocked IP addresses.

To block an IP address

1. In Store Manager, click on the Risk Tools under the order settings column.

2. In the Risk Tools Manager, click on the IP Blocking link.

3. Type the IP address or addresses you would like to block in the first column and then click on the Add button.

FIGURE 14.9

Each order will include the IP address of the computer the customer used to place the order.

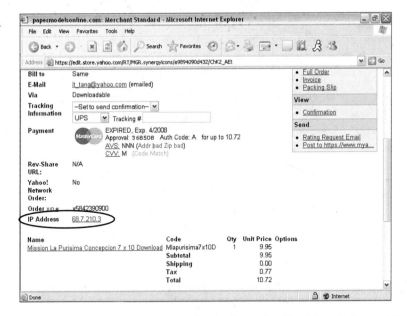

For further investigation, you can also look up the IP address before adding it to the blocked list. Doing so will reveal the Internet service provider (ISP) the IP address belongs to. The ISP information is useful if you decide to contact the ISP for additional assistance or warning.

Managing Inventory

Customers expect that when they place an order, it will arrive within the promised time frame. Getting it there earlier than expected will even make the customer happier, thus providing a greater buying experience. Providing a great shopping experience will not only earn you a loyal customer, but that customer will recommend your online store to her friends and family. Keeping inventory in stock and keeping an eye on low inventory levels will eliminate delays in shipping and reduce returns from customers who received a particular product too late.

Keeping an accurate and up-to-date inventory list will help you keep your business running smoothly. It will also help you view which items are selling well and which items may need additional exposure or a reduction in pricing.

Your inventory management procedure will depend on the number of products you offer, the size of your company, and the volume of products you are selling.

Here's a list of things to consider when planning your inventory management procedures.

■ **Identification**: How will you identify each product? Will it be by name, SKU number, bar code, price, or your own unique code?

■ **Documentation**: Make sure the procedures are well documented. This will ensure that new employees will have a reference and repeat the same procedures. Include procedures such as shipping, product holds, handling returns, and documenting orders.

■ **Training**: If you have more than one person helping you, make sure that person is properly trained using the documented procedures.

■ **Accountability**: If you have employees, make sure they are accountable for their mistakes. If they do make mistakes, make sure they are quickly rectified, or have another training session with that employee.

■ **Tracking**: Will you be able to track which item was shipped to which customer? Having a good documentation and tracking system will give you control of your inventory.

■ **Re-evaluate**: Take a look at your procedures periodically. Make sure your process is still effective, and determine whether any improvements can be made. Ask your assistants or employees if they have any recommendations or changes on how the process can be streamlined or improved.

■ **Monitor**: Monitor the process to ensure all the steps are followed. Any missteps can cause the whole process to fail, thus making the tracking of inventory impossible.

If you rely on a third party to stock and ship your products, make sure they have enough inventory. Constantly monitor their current inventory levels and make sure they contact you when the inventory researches a certain threshold level. Also, if you are using the Inventory Manager, make sure the data is updated.

> **tip** If you rely on a third party to supply your product line, make sure you have a backup supplier just in case your original supplier cannot come through. Never rely on what are called "sole sources" for your business. Not being able to meet the demands of your customers can mean the end of your business. Remember those newsgroups we spoke about in Chapter 11, "Basic Marketing—Promoting Your Yahoo! Store for Free." Bad reviews can be detrimental to your reputation.

Restocking Inventory

As mentioned in Chapter 10, "Setting Up Your Yahoo! Store Order Settings," Merchant Solutions has a built-in

Inventory Management System that will allow you to set alerts when a particular item in inventory reaches a certain threshold you set. This will allow you adequate time to restock your inventory.

Take a look at your product purchase volumes and rates so you can have a better idea of how much more inventory you need to purchase. Not having enough stock will require you to frequently reorder inventory. Having too much stock will require more capital, and it may stay on the shelves longer than expected and take up valuable space.

> **caution** Unless you're making your own products or are selling downloadable goods, make sure you know how much inventory your suppliers have and how long it will take for you to restock your inventory. Although you order your products in advance, it doesn't mean you will receive them on time.

Viewing Site Statistics

Part of your daily or weekly duties is to view the web statistics of your site. Yahoo! generates and supplies a large number of site statistics that reflect activity on your storefront. You will want to know things such as how many visitors came to your website; how many visitors came this month compared to last month or same month last year; which products are being viewed the most; which products are being viewed the least; how effective your marketing campaign is; whether the newspaper advertisement you paid for drove additional traffic to your site; and whether you received any traffic from search engines, and if so which ones and which keywords shoppers used to find you. All these questions can be answered by reviewing your site statistics.

To view site statistics

1. From the Manage My Service Control Panel, click on the Store Manager Control Panel link.

2. Under the Statistics column as seen in Figure 14.10, you can click on any of the links such as Page View and References to generate the particular stats report you want to view.

So how will these statistics help your business? For example, when viewing the number of visitors to your site, you will be able to view how well your site is doing over a period of time. This will give you insight on how much traffic your site is getting. Is the site traffic increasing or decreasing? Is the marketing campaign working or not working? Are you receiving the expected Return on

Investment (ROI) on that particular advertising campaign? If the data is mined properly, you will be able to answer all these questions.

Let's take a look at a few statistical reports from PaperModelsOnline.com.

FIGURE 14.10
Site statistics are available under the Statistics column in the Store Manager Control Panel.

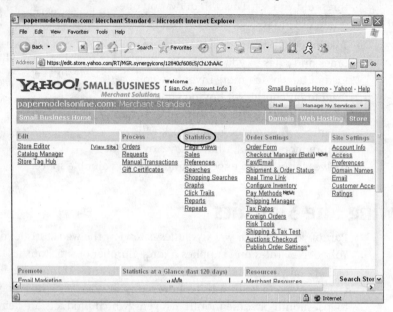

Search Engine Keyword Report

You can view which keywords or keyword phrases your customers are using to search for your site. As shown in Figure 14.11, you see a list of keywords used and how many times that keyword was used. The search engine keyword report is crucial if you are implementing a search engine optimization strategy. You can see which keywords you successfully optimized for and which keywords need some additional optimization.

Referring URLs Report

Another powerful site activity report is the referring URL report, as shown in Figure 14.12. This will give you a list of other websites that are sending you traffic. If link trading is part of your strategy, this will show you a list of which sites are sending you traffic, and how much. This can help you decide where to place their reciprocal link, or determine which sites you need to renegotiate with for better link placement.

You can also find out who is linking to your website by going to www.google.com and typing in "link:www.yourdomain.com".

Visits	Orders	Revenue	Revenue per Visit	Referring URL
13				Yahoo search for paper models
6				Yahoo search for free cardstock models
5				Yahoo search for san juan bautista mission kit
4				Yahoo search for alamo paper model
4				Yahoo search for globe theatre card model
4				Yahoo search for models of globe theatre
3				Yahoo search for "shakespeare" "globe theatre" paper
3				Yahoo search for Washington monument model kit
3				Yahoo search for free paper model
3				Yahoo search for models of the alamo
3				Yahoo search for paper Globe Model
3				Yahoo search for theatre models
3				Yahoo search with unknown query terms
3				Yahoo search with unknown query terms
2				Yahoo search for free paper models
2				Yahoo search for grade 7 globe theatre
2				Yahoo search for grade 7 globe theatre
2				Yahoo search for 3D paper models
2				Yahoo search for 3D printed paper model
2				Yahoo search for 3d model san antonio mission
2				Yahoo search for 3d paper model of the alamo
2				Yahoo search for 3d paper models

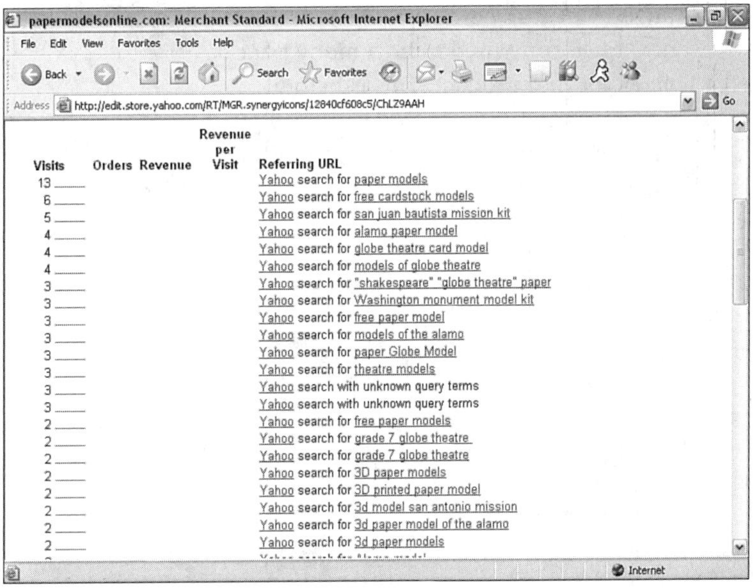

FIGURE 14.11
You can view reports such as which search engines are sending you traffic and what keywords customers are using to find your site.

Visits	Orders	Revenue	Revenue per Visit	Referring URL
256	8	126.60	0.49	http://www.yahoo.com/ (Many pages) [details]
61	16	250.20	4.10	http://www.google.com/ (Many pages) [details]
19	2	39.90	2.10	http://www.msn.com/ (Many pages) [details]
17				http://store.yahoo.com/ (1 page) [details]
16	1	19.95	1.25	http://order.store.yahoo.com/ (3 pages) [details]
7				http://rds.yahoo.com/ (7 pages) [details]
6	1	9.95	1.66	http://www.dogpile.com/ (5 pages) [details]
6				http://www.altavista.com/ (6 pages) [details]
3	3	37.85	12.62	http://www.brandsonsale.com/ (2 pages) [details]
3	2	34.90	11.63	http://aolsearch.aol.com/ (3 pages) [details]
3	1	11.95	3.98	http://search.earthlink.net/ (2 pages) [details]
3				http://www.google.ca/ (1 page) [details]
3				http://www.google.co.uk/ (2 pages) [details]
3				http://www.jekoo.com/ (2 pages) [details]
2	1	24.95	12.47	http://www.mywebsearch.com/ (2 pages) [details]
2				http://2log.com/ (2 pages) [details]
2				http://images.search.yahoo.com/ (1 page) [details]
2				http://webferret.search.com/ (2 pages) [details]
2				http://www.alltheweb.com/ (1 page) [details]
2				http://www.google.at/ (1 page) [details]
2				http://www.overture.com/ (1 page) [details]
1	1	42.90	42.90	http://www.bossfeed.com/ (1 page) [details]

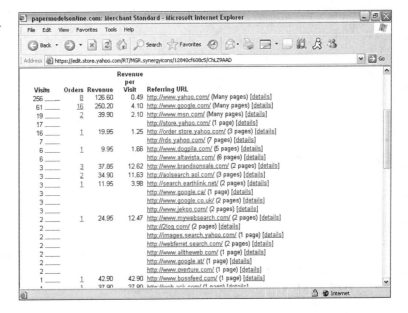

FIGURE 14.12
Referring URL reports can help you determine the success of your link exchange campaign. The report will list websites that link to your page.

Page Views Report

You can view the number of page views for individual pages as seen in Figure 14.13, or you can get a summary of all page views for the entire site. Page view reports are great for calculating the ROI of a particular page. For product

pages, you can view how many sales were
generated compared to how many page
views for that product. This is helpful
when determining whether you need to
make changes to the product page to
increase its sales rate.

tip When you first view your
stats, create a baseline
report and date it. This will allow
you to create your own statistical
reports on the progress of your site
for future use.

FIGURE 14.13
Page view
reports show
which pages are
generating the
most amount of
traffic and
which pages are
generating the
least amount of
traffic. The
report will
display the
exact number of
page views for
each individual
page.

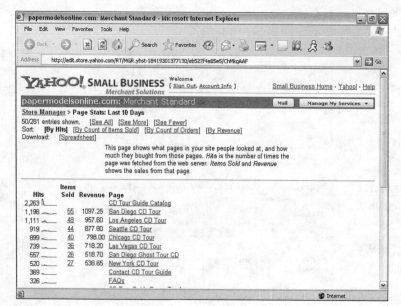

Generating Sales Reports

Besides generating site statistics, you can also generate sales statistics. Want to
view how many orders were generated for each product? How much revenue
was produced from that product? How much revenue was generated yester-
day, last week, last month, or even in the last 365 days? You can even compare a certain month to the same month last year. Merchant Solutions also
has tools to present your data in a graph format.

Let's take a look at a few sample sales reports.

Monthly Store Activity Report

As seen in Figure 14.14, this report gives you a quick glance of monthly sales
statistics. The report is displayed in a table format by month. Although the

default report is by month, you can also switch to weekly and daily view. For each month, you can view the following:

- Number of page views
- Number of customers that came to the site
- Average page view per customer
- Total number of orders
- Total amount of sales
- How many items were sold
- Average order amount

The Monthly Store Activity Report is a great way to quickly glance at how well your site is performing.

FIGURE 14.14

The Monthly Store Activity Report can give you a quick glance of sales statistics. This is a great tool to view sales data over a period of time.

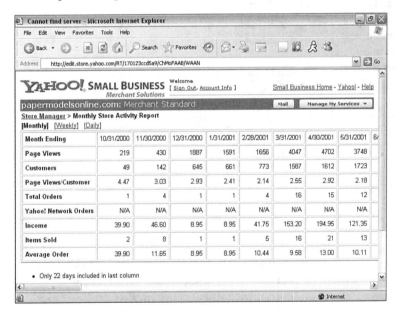

Month Ending	10/31/2000	11/30/2000	12/31/2000	1/31/2001	2/28/2001	3/31/2001	4/30/2001	5/31/2001	6/
Page Views	219	430	1887	1591	1656	4047	4702	3748	
Customers	49	142	645	661	773	1587	1612	1723	
Page Views/Customer	4.47	3.03	2.93	2.41	2.14	2.55	2.92	2.18	
Total Orders	1	4	1	1	4	16	15	12	
Yahoo! Network Orders	N/A	N/A	N/A	N/A	N/A	N/A	N/A	N/A	
Income	39.90	46.60	8.95	8.95	41.75	153.20	194.95	121.35	
Items Sold	2	8	1	1	5	16	21	13	
Average Order	39.90	11.65	8.95	8.95	10.44	9.58	13.00	10.11	

- Only 22 days included in last column

To view the Monthly Store Activity Report

1. From the Manage My Service Control Panel, click on the Store Manager Control Panel link.
2. Under the Statistics column, click on the Reports link.

Sales by Product Report

You can view sales statistics for every item in your store, as seen in Figure 14.15. The sales report will list all your items ranked by the number of orders.

It will also display the total amount generated for each item. This is a great tool to show how well your items are selling. If an item falls below expectations, you may want to consider repositioning the item onto a page with a higher page view.

To view the Sales by Product Report

1. From the Manage My Service Control Panel, click on the Store Manager Control Panel link.

2. Under the Statistics column, click on the Sales link.

FIGURE 14.15

The Sales by Product Report will display all the products available in your store and the revenue generated for each product. The report is ranked by the number of products sold.

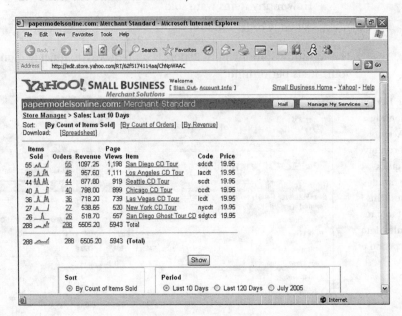

Managing your workflow will keep your business running smoothly and keep your customers satisfied. In this chapter we discussed how to process orders, manage your inventory, and prevent losing revenue to fraudulent orders. In the next chapter, we'll discuss customer service and tips to avoid getting bad reviews or returned products. We'll also discuss how Yahoo! can be your help desk.

Customer Service and Shipping

Customer Service—Keeping Your Customers Happy

If you don't have an inexpensive or unique product, how will you separate yourself from your competitors? One of the ways to stand out from the rest of the pack is to provide not only a great buying experience, but the ability to cater to your customer needs. Buyers do not base their buying decisions solely on price or availability. They also base their decision on how comfortable they feel doing business with you. Can you answer their questions in a timely manner? Can you deliver the product in the promised time frame? Will you be there when they need assistance with your product? Will you stand by your product if there is an issue with it?

With all the advances in technology, customers expect more than before when it comes to customer service. Communication tools such as instant messaging, email, cell phones, wireless Internet, personal digital assistants (PDAs), text phones, and more have given businesses the ability to respond quickly. It is assumed that if you have an online business, you have access to one or more of these communication tools.

Free Info   Download the free informative article titled "Sugar & Spice" at www.MyEcommerceSuccess.com.

The 24-hour Rule

Your customers expect that if they send you an email or leave you a voicemail, you will respond within 24 hours at the latest. Not responding within 24 hours can send the wrong message to your customers. It will make them wonder if you are still in business, a fly-by-night company, or whether you just don't really care about customer service.

If you need additional time to respond to an inquiry, just let your customer know. They'll appreciate the notice as long as they know you are working on the issue. Also let them know when they will hear from you again.

When you do respond, make sure you completely answer all their questions and concerns. Not responding to all their questions will delay the purchasing process and may drive them straight to your competitors. You'll never know if one of the questions you didn't answer is a deal breaker.

tip Be sure to have a contact form or contact email link on your website, and set up your email to auto-respond to the customer. An auto responder is an email reply automatically sent to customers when they send email to you. You can include a message that you have received the email and a customer service representative will contact them within a given time period. This is also a great tool when you are on vacation and will not be able to respond to them within 24 hours.

When you do use an auto responder, make sure you take that opportunity to market to them. Throw in your latest special or value added offer in the auto responder. You might make a sale right then and there. And don't forget an FAQ page (frequently asked questions) where the merchant answers (and updates) the most frequently asked questions. This may be enough to get a shopper to place an order and will help keep support costs down.

Answering Questions

More traffic and exposure to your website usually means more questions and inquiries about your products. Answering emails and phone calls can literally take hours out of your day. Each inquiry is unique and needs to be crafted for that particular customer.

Here are some tips to help reduce customer inquiries:

- If you start receiving the same questions over and over, create an online knowledge base or FAQ section.

  And, try to fix it! Add more information, diagrams, flow charts, or even a video.

- Create a spreadsheet of answers to common questions for you to cut and paste into the emails.

- Be as descriptive as possible on your product pages.

- Create an audio or video "How To" on your website.

- List resources of other websites that may help them.

- Also, if the question relates to a specific product, make sure the answer is included on revisions to text of that product page. Some buyers will ask questions, but others will just leave and you can lose sales. Rule #1—provide all info to allow shoppers to make a purchase decision.

Making the Call—Get Personal

Email is a fast and efficient communication tool, but it has become very impersonal. Whatever happened to the days of meeting clients and doing business over a handshake? Although this hasn't completely disappeared, it has become less frequent. Online stores have even made it more impersonal because your customers are not going to a physical store and meeting someone in person before purchasing a product.

So take the extra step and get personal. Sometimes it's faster to speak to someone then compose an email. You will be amazed at your customers' reactions if you pick up the phone and call them in person. You will not only close the sale, but maybe up-sell your products while you have them on the phone (up-sell and cross-sell!). With inexpensive and unlimited long-distance calling plans, it has become cheaper to call across the country. If you have a cell phone, almost every cell phone calling plan comes with free long distance. Also, consider acquiring a toll-free 800 number. There is a cost to these numbers, but they lend credibility to sites and make your small business seem larger.

Here are some customer service tips to follow:

- Respond in a timely manner
- Under-promise and over-deliver

- Be courteous when speaking to customers
- Have a can-do attitude
- Diffuse anger by apologizing
- Ask if there is anything else you can do for the customer
- Address the person by name during the conversation
- Know your product
- Make sure the product arrives in good condition
- Show your appreciation by thanking customers for their order
- If you get too many email questions, create a FAQ page and address the issues

Under-promise—Over-deliver

Receiving your order before the promised time frame is like getting a birthday or Christmas present before the actual date, especially if it's an item your customers can hardly wait to get their hands on. For example, suppose your regular shipping option takes 5–7 business days to receive. You might want to ship the item Priority so the customer will receive the package within 2–3 business days.

Another way to under-promise and over-deliver is to add a bonus to your package. Throw in something extra for the customer. Find something inexpensive that complements the product and send it with the package. This will surely put a smile on your customer's face. If you do decide to give a little something extra, include a note. This will let them know that you went the extra mile for them.

Problem Resolution

Once in a while you'll get that customer that you just can't seem to satisfy, no matter what you do. So what do you do when you get that angry, irate, and unsatisfied customer? Remember the old saying, "The customer is always right"? Even though he may not be right, you can still make him believe that he is.

Here are some techniques to follow when handling these difficult customers:

- Listen to the customer.
- Apologize for not being satisfied with your product.
- Show them you understand the issue.

- Own up to the situation.
- Thank them for their feedback and say that you value their opinion.
- Be calm. Do not escalate the situation with your own emotions.
- Ask them what you can do for them. You may still be able to keep them as a customer by introducing them to another product that they would like better.

Being able to handle difficult customers is key to customer service. The last thing you want is for the customer to post an unsatisfied report on newsgroups or blogs or give you a bad rating. One bad review can scare other potential customers away.

Remember

- An angry customer tells up to 20 other people about a bad experience.
- A satisfied customer shares good experiences with 9–12 people.
- It costs five times as much to get a customer as it does to keep one.
- Customers will spend up to 10% more for the same product if they receive better service.
- 68% of customer loss is because they were mishandled.

Customer Feedback—Yahoo! Ratings

As discussed in Chapter 13, "Marketing and Merchandising Your Store Using Yahoo! Tools," Yahoo! merchant ratings and reviews are based on a one- to five-star scale. Your ability to provide excellent customer service and a good product will be reflected in your rating. Going the extra mile for your customer will help raise your Yahoo! rating from three stars to four stars and even five stars. The merchant rating system only considers ratings you have received within the last six months, so any ratings received more than six months ago will not be calculated.

As seen in Figure 15.1, each merchant has an Overall rating as well as five component ratings: Price, Shipping Options, Delivery, Ease of Purchase, and Customer Service. New merchants will need to have at least five individual ratings before the ratings are displayed. A Not Yet Rated icon will appear if the minimum requirement has not yet been met. All reviews typically appear within 2–4 business days.

Participation in merchant rating is not mandatory unless you are planning on submitting your products to Yahoo! Shopping.

To enable customer ratings

1. From Store Manager, click on the Order Form link under the Order Settings column.

2. Scroll down until you see the Customer Rating section. Select Yes in the Enabled drop-down list.

3. Click Done. This will return you to the Store Manager.

4. Click on the Publish Orders Settings link under the Order Settings Column to make the change live.

FIGURE 15.1

Yahoo! merchant ratings are based on a one- to five-star scale. This example from PaperModels Online.com shows an over-all rating of four and a half stars out of five from 50 individual ratings.

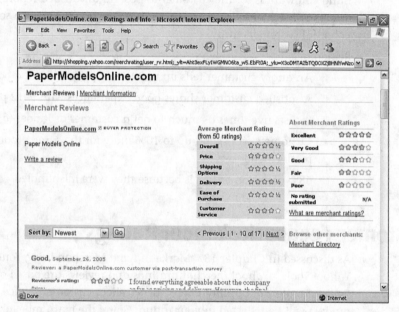

Often, customers make mistakes or give a merchant a rating that is lower than the merchant would expect. Merchants cannot dispute ratings unless they are suspect for a number of reasons. However, merchants can and should try to contact the customer to discuss the bad rating. This is an opportunity to learn and possibly improve or refine text on your site to set expectations properly. At times shoppers may have made a mistake and not be aware they gave a low rating. Merchants can then resubmit a rating request email from the Order Manager and the latest (hopefully better) ranking will replace the former rating.

Shipping Your Products

Packaging and getting your products ready to ship is one of the most labor-intensive duties. In Chapter 10, "Setting Up Your Yahoo! Store Order Settings," we discussed choosing your shipping provider and setting up your shipping options. Now let's take a look at how to package and ship your products.

Packaging Tips

Picking the right box: Pick a box with enough room for adding cushioning material. Depending on the size of your products, you will most likely need a variety of different-sized boxes. Check with your shipping provider to see whether they offer free packaging material. If so, this will surely reduce the cost of shipping your products. If not, buy some boxes.

caution Try to avoid reusing old boxes with markings and labels on them. They look unprofessional and used. This could send the wrong message about your company and product.

Choosing the right box will also reduce shipping cost. Depending on which shipping provider and method of shipping you use, most likely the size of the box will be part of the calculation when determining shipping cost. The bigger the box, the heavier it is and the more it will cost.

Cushioning: Place cushioning around your items. Close and shake the box to see whether you have enough cushioning material around your items. Add additional newspaper and bubble wrap if you hear the product shift.

If your items are very fragile, consider double-cushioning your items. For example, you may want to bubble wrap your item and then add additional Styrofoam around the item to keep it from shifting. Remember, a broken item will have a domino effect: Not only will the product be returned, but you will have to reship the item, delay the shipping time, lose revenue on additional shipping, and lose revenue on the broken item if it cannot be returned or replaced.

Sealing your package: Use special packaging tape to seal your box. Choose clear or brown tape. Make sure all the seams and openings are taped. Avoid using string or twine because the loose material can get caught in the mail processing equipment. Place words on the shipping box such as "Fragile," "Electronics," "This Side Up," "Glass," or other labels that might help with special handling.

Shipping Tips

Verifying the shipping address: Every delivery address should be verified before the package is shipped. The last thing you want is your item to be shipped to the wrong location. If that happens, it will be virtually impossible to retrieve the package. The great news is that the United States Postal Service

(USPS), FedEx, and United Parcel Service (UPS) have online tools to validate the shipping address.

Signature confirmation: Another option to confirm that your item was received, and by whom, is to have the shipping company require a signature from the recipient. This is additional proof that the item was received if a dispute ever arises. If a signature is required, the shipping company will not leave the item at the doorstep if someone is not there to sign for the package. The shipping company will make additional attempts to obtain the signature, or the customer may choose to go to the shipping center to pick up the package. We suggest that you use discretion when using the signature confirmation option. Most people who order are at work with no one to sign for the parcel at the home address. The package gets returned and the customer gets angry.

Schedule a pickup: Making multiple daily trips to the shipping center can become mundane and time-consuming. Instead of dropping off the packages, you can schedule to have the shipping company pick up the packages, or take all of the packages at the end of the day.

Tracking Packages

When sending packages, make sure they can be tracked. Being able to track packages will reduce emails and phone calls asking "When will I receive my order?" You can also insert the tracking number into your shipping confirmation emails. This will put the responsibility of the tracking of the package on the customer.

When using UPS or FedEx, tracking is included with every package. Just go to the company website, as seen in Figure 15.2, and enter the tracking number to view the status of your package. An added benefit is that if you set up an account with FedEx, UPS, or USPS, the labels print right out of your printer. Just slap them on the box and drop them off.

For United States Postal Service (USPS) mail, tracking is available for an extra fee. If you are planning on using USPS, consider using the Endicia Internet Postage software (Endicia.com). Tracking is free for Priority Mail and discounted for all other packages. Endicia will allow you to print postage for all your mail right from your computer. A 30-day trial version of the software is available from the company's website. But the post office only provides tracking at the destination. In-route tracking is no longer available as it is with FedEx and UPS.

FIGURE 15.2

If you are using
United Parcel
Service (UPS),
you can track
your packages
by entering the
tracking number
in the tracking
search box on
their website.

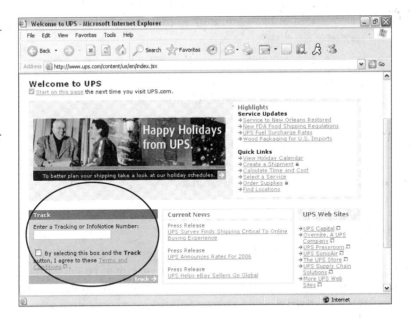

Basic Record Keeping

Running a successful online business requires keeping accurate records and up-to-date financial information. Having a clear picture of your company profits and losses will allow you to make strategic financial decisions.

So why do you need to keep good records? Besides for paying your taxes, you will also need to create profit and loss statements, retrieve customer data, use the information to generate more sales, manage inventory levels, calculate ROI, pay employees, and so forth. You don't want to wait until the end of the year when you are doing your income taxes to find out that you are in the negative. Having a good record keeping and accounting system will allow you make strategic decisions in a near-real-time basis. Having updated information will depend on how often you update your accounting system.

A typical record keeping system includes three types of records: inventory, customer, and financial.

Inventory Records

You want to be able to track when you received your products, how many products you currently have, how much they cost, when you sold them, and how much you sold them for.

Here's a list of fields you may want to collect for your inventory management system:

- Name of item
- Description of item
- Item model or serial number
- Cost of item
- Date item was purchased
- Date item was sold
- Amount item was sold for

Customer Records

Establishing a good customer management system is as important as having a good inventory management system. Having a good and updated system will not only help you quickly retrieve customer data, but mining the specific data such as email addresses will help increase future sales and help put together email marketing campaigns. You will also be able to view buying trends and even use the list to solicit future sales.

Here's a list of fields you may want to collect for your customer management system:

- Customer name
- Customer contact information (mailing address, shipping address, email, phone)
- Item(s) purchased
- Quantity of item purchase
- Date item was purchased
- Payment method and payment information
- Date item was shipped
- Shipping method and cost

Exporting Order and Customer Data

Merchant Solutions allows you to export your order information into various file formats ("export" is not available to Merchant Starter merchants) such as Excel, XML, Access, Generic CSV, and more:

1. From the Store Manager, click on the Orders link under the Process column.

2. Enter your Yahoo! Security Key.

3. Scroll down until you see the Export options, as seen in Figure 15.3.

4. Enter the range of orders you would like to export.

5. Select the export file format from the drop-down menu.

6. Click on the Export button.

FIGURE 15.3

You can export a range of orders into various file formats such as Excel, XML, Access, Generic CSV, and more.

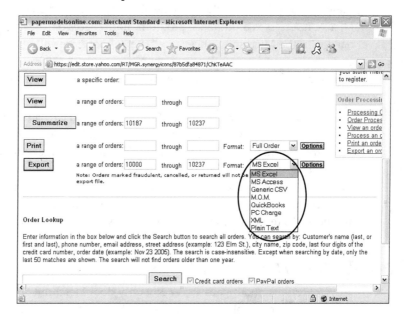

Financial Records

A good financial records system will help alleviate frustration when filing your tax returns. It will also help answer IRS questions relating to your financial statements. Try to maintain daily records. You do not want to have all these invoices and receipts piling up in a shoe box. That will only make it more difficult to record all your transactions. The longer you wait, the more likely you will forget to record some of the invoices or receipts. Do it while it's fresh in your head.

Here's a list of items you may want to collect for your financial management system:

- Receipts of all your business-related purchases and expenses (office supplies, equipment, shipping expenses, meals, travel, transportation, rent, hosting, Internet access, and so on)

- Bank statements

- Invoices of all purchases

- Sales receipts and invoices for all items sold

Accounting Software

You can hire an accountant to handle all your accounting needs, or if you are the do-it-yourself type, you can use software to help you manage all these records. Microsoft Excel and Access are great software tools to help you with these accounting tasks. Microsoft Excel is a spreadsheet program and Microsoft Access is a database program. Both pieces of software come packaged with the Microsoft Office Suite. The Yahoo! store will allow you to export customer and order data that can then be used with MS Excel or Access. You can create custom reports and advanced calculations with these software programs.

As discussed in Chapter 7, "Tools of the Trade," you can also purchase business accounting software such as QuickBooks, Microsoft Money, Quicken, or Peachtree. Business accounting software will allow you to enter customer data, generate invoices, pay bills, and even calculate revenue and expenses. Take a look at each piece of software and see what's right for your business. Using business accounting software will help you better manage your business finances. It's recommended that you use business accounting software.

Yahoo! As a Partner Help Desk

Have questions about your store? Not only does Merchant Solutions have a great online help tool with hundreds of FAQs, but Yahoo! also provides 24/7 live customer support. Think of it as your own help desk provider. Whether you have questions on store functionality or how to add an image to a product page, Customer Care is there to help. Having live help around the clock can be crucial to your online business. After all, your store is open 24 hours a day, 7 days a week.

Now that's a partner!

Getting Help Online

If your question is not an emergency, you can contact Customer Care by email via the online form. Merchant Solutions will respond within 24 hours.

To email technical support

1. Go to smallbusiness.yahoo.com/contactus/.
2. Select the appropriate category and topic and then click Continue.
3. Type your question in the form and click the Send button.

Getting Help on the Phone

You can also contact Yahoo! Merchant Solutions Technical Support by telephone.

To get the technical support phone number

1. Go to smallbusiness.yahoo.com/contactus/.

2. Select your appropriate category and topic and then click Continue.

3. A list of FAQs related to the topic will appear. If the FAQs do not answer your question, click on the Contact Us Link.

4. Scroll to the bottom and click on Contact Us by Telephone link. A page will appear with the technical support phone number.

Congratulations! If you followed the advice in this book, you're ready to *"Launch Your Yahoo! Business"*. Once you have had some experience with your Yahoo! store, pick up the companion to this book, *Succeeding with Your Yahoo! Business*, which will help you establish a full-time eCommerce business of your own. And don't forget to visit our website www.MyEcommerceSuccess.com and register to receive the free downloads and more that are listed in the chapters of this book.

Part VI

Appendixes

Daily, Weekly, and Monthly Tasks

When running an eBusiness, it's easy to forget the day-to-day tasks that need to be done to keep your eBusiness on track. Let's face it. You've put a lot of work into building a foundation for your new enterprise. Keeping that foundation solid is an important task in making your eBusiness a success. So, here is a *Do List* of activities that you should do on a daily, weekly, and monthly basis.

Daily Tasks

■ **Check for New Orders**: New order notifications can be sent to an email account or fax machine (Standard and Professional members only). Check your email or fax machine frequently to ensure prompt processing.

■ **Process Current Orders**: Once you receive the order, you will need to process the payment. The sooner you process the order, the sooner the funds will be transferred into your bank account.

■ **Ship Orders**: All physical goods will need to be shipped. You can take the packages to the mail center or schedule for a pickup time.

■ **Send Shipping Status Emails**: Once the package is sent, a notification email should be sent to the customer. A shipping tracking number should also be included if available. This can also be automated by the merchant in Shipment and Order Status page.

■ **Answer All Emails and Phone Calls**: Customer emails and phone calls such as calls about orders, questions about the products, shipments not received or late, and double charges should be returned daily.

■ **Address Online Newsgroups**: Monitor and participate in any online newsgroups you belong to.

■ **Pursue Sales Leads**: Follow up and contact any potential sales leads.

Weekly Tasks

■ **Monitor Inventory**: Monitoring and fulfilling inventory levels will ensure prompt product delivery. Merchants can set up their Yahoo! stores to send them email inventory alerts when inventory reaches a certain level depending on velocity of orders, so they don't have to do this all the time.

■ **Purchase New Products**: Purchase new products to ensure product availability.

■ **Add New Photos and Product Descriptions**: Photograph and write a product description for each new product.

■ **Add New Products**: Once you have purchased your new product, photographed it, and written a description, you will then need to add it to the online store.

- **Add New Items to the Home Page**: You may want to add new items or rotate items that are on sale on the home page.
- **Pursue Link Exchanges**: Exchanging links with other related websites will help improve online traffic and boost search engine ranking.
- **Monitor the Competition**: Monitor the competition for price increases or decreases and online web strategies.
- **Monitor Pay-Per-Click Advertising Campaigns**: Monitor the ROI (return on investment) of your product or keyword advertising. This will help you determine which keywords and products are not performing.
- **Analyze Web Stats**: Analyze the web traffic to your store. See which product pages are most popular, view which keywords visitors are using to find your website via the search engines, and view the results of your advertising efforts.
- **Analyze Product Purchase Rates**: Create reports to see trends on product performance.
- **Add to Blog**: Add content to your online web journal.
- **Submit Product Feed**: Submit your products or update your product feed to other product search engines.
- **Contact Affiliates**: Contact other potential affiliates to see whether they would be willing to promote your product or services.
- **Deposit Offline Order Funds**: Some customers will not want to use their credit cards online. You will need to make a trip to the bank and deposit their checks.

Monthly Tasks

- **Research New Products**: Research new products and product trends to include in your store.
- **Update Accounting Records**: Update accounting database with new orders and expenditures.
- **Keep up with the Industry**: Be informed with industry changes and updates.
- **Send E-newsletter**: Compose and send monthly e-newsletter done in-house or through a third party such as ConstantContact.

- **Contribute to Other Online Newsletters**: Contributing to other online newsletters will create additional exposure to your online store.

- **Pay Bills**: Pay monthly business-related bills including utilities, rent, employees, office supplies, and so on.

- **Add to Pay-per-click Accounts**: Add additional funds to pay-per-click accounts.

- **Analyze Web Statistics**: Analyze web statistics and logs for long term trends.

- **Update Customer Contact List**: Update your customer contact list.

- **Monitor Your Offline Advertisements**: Just like online advertisement, you will need to also monitor offline advertisements for ROI.

- **Pay Required Taxes**: To avoid penalties, make sure you pay your fair share of taxes.

- **Update Your Business Plan**: Keep your business plan updated in order to keep goals focused.

- **Submit to Search Engines**: Submit your website to search engines.

- **Add New Content**: Add additional keyword heavy content to help improve search engine ranking. Also refine sales copy to improve close rate.

- **Do Your Networking**: Attend local networking meetings such as the Chamber of Commerce.

Important Resources on the Web

This appendix provides a list of Net-based resources that will broaden your understanding of eCommerce and provide valuable information that will help you succeed in your online business. These eBusiness resources will help your growing enterprise compete by using sound business practices, establishing business and marketing relationships, building product and service quality programs, and entering international markets.

The resources listed here take a variety of formats. Many are standard web addresses whereas others are mailing lists. To subscribe to the mailing lists, simply send an email to the address listed, unless instructed otherwise.

Yahoo! Store Resources

My Ecommerce Success

www.myecommercesuccess.com

MyEcommerceSuccess.com offers comprehensive Yahoo! store resources including training videos, articles, development companies, books, seminars, newsletters, and eMarketing strategies.

Solid Cactus

www.solidcactus.com

Yahoo!'s premier development partner. Solid Cactus has developed hundreds of Yahoo! stores.

Y-Times Publications

www.ytimes.com

Y-Times Publications offers books on learning RTML as well as Yahoo! store tips and tricks.

Email Discussion Lists

E-Tailer Digest

www.etailersdigest.com/subscribe.htm

E-Tailer's Digest is a resource for retail on the Net and is published in a moderated digest form every Monday, Wednesday, and Friday. The E-Tailer Digest's topics include any and all subjects that pertain to retailing.

FrankelBiz

www.robfrankel.com/frankelbiz/form.html

FrankelBiz is the Web's only listserv devoted exclusively to doing business on the Web instead of talking about it. List members exchange reciprocal discounts, offer business leads, and do business with one another. Sponsors offer products and services at discounts to members.

GB Internet Marketing

www.digitalnation.co.uk/subscribe.htm

The GB Internet Marketing discussion list deals with all aspects of Internet marketing relevant to the United Kingdom.

GLOBAL_PROMOTE

join-global_promote@gs4.revnet.com

This list is a forum for the discussion of issues relating to sales and marketing in the worldwide Internet marketplace.

The List of Marketing Lists

www.nsns.com/MouseTracks/tloml.html

A comprehensive directory of marketing discussion lists.

IESSlist

majordomo@ix.entrepreneurs.net

IESS (Internet Entrepreneurs Support Service) is a discussion group for entrepreneurs and businesses doing business on the Internet.

The Best Internet Marketing Forums

www.ozemedia.com/forums.htm

If you want to rapidly increase and enhance your online presence, you should become an active member of forums or discussion boards. The best of them are great places to spread the gospel, in a quiet way, about your service or product.

Retailer-News

www.retailernews.com

The Retailer-News Digest mailing list is a moderated discussion list for retail business owners, managers, and salespeople.

SMBIZ

mail.abanet.org/archives/smbiz.html

The Small Business discussion list is for all small business owners, workers, marketers, and developers. To subscribe, send the message subscribe.

eBusiness Publications

American Demographics Magazine

www.demographics.com

Online reproduction of the print version of *American Demographics* magazine. The best demographic information online. A necessity for any good marketing plan.

Boardwatch Magazine

boardwatch.internet.com

Guide to Internet access and the World Wide Web.

ClickZ

www.clickz.com

This column is published each business day and includes an eclectic mixture of online marketing news, opinions, and interviews.

CNET

www.cnet.com

As well as carrying all the latest technical news online, CNET publishes a weekly summary that provides links to all the major Internet stories from the previous week.

Entrepreneur Magazine

www.EntrepreneurMag.com

A wide range of articles and suggestions for starting, managing, and maintaining a small business.

Fast Company

www.fastcompany.com

Contains plenty of articles about emerging businesses. The website is well organized, expansive, and covers up-to-date issues for today's entrepreneur.

INC. ONLINE

www.inc.com

The award-winning web magazine for growing companies.

Interactive Week

www.interactive-week.com

Covers a variety of aspects of the Internet and interactive technology.

Net Magazine

www.netmag.co.uk

Popular European Internet magazine.

Small Business Journal

www.tsbj.com

The *Small Business Journal* magazine has tons of small business articles and information.

Web Commerce Today

www.wilsonweb.com/wct

Monthly email newsletter on selling products directly over the Internet.

Wired Magazine

www.wired.com

Internet culture and business magazine.

eCommerce Times

www.ecommercetimes.com

The eCommerce Times offers industry strategies for online merchants and provides daily news, articles, and research.

Internet Retailer

www.internetretailer.com

Also offers industry strategies for online merchants and provide daily news, articles, and research.

SEO Chat

www.seochat.com

Search engine optimization news and tools.

General Resources

Domain Name Availability

www.networksolutions.com

Checks the availability of a domain name.

Emarketer

www.emarketer.com

This site aims to be the definitive online marketing resource. It includes news, statistics, and step-by-step guides to succeeding online. A weekly newsletter also is available.

Incorporation and Trademarks

www.corpcreations.com

Incorporation and trademark services online (for all 50 states plus offshore).

NUA Internet Surveys

www.nua.ie/surveys/moreinfo.html

NUA publishes a weekly email newsletter that summarizes all the latest Internet surveys and statistics. This newsletter is an invaluable resource if you want to know who's online and what they're buying.

Wilson Web

www.wilsonweb.com

This site contains a wealth of links to articles relating to every aspect of web commerce. Much of the information is free, although some areas are accessible by paying subscribers only.

Delphi Forums

delphiforums.com

Delphi Forums is one of the largest discussion boards on the Net and has more than 500,000 individual discussion forums to participate in.

Yahoo! Groups

groups.yahoo.com

Yahoo! Groups is a good resource for finding mailing lists that relate to your product or service. It is also one the easiest ways for companies to communicate with prospects and customers on the Internet.

Lsoft

lsoft.com/lists/listref.html

Lsoft has the CataList, the official catalog of LISTSERV lists on the Net. CataList has tens of thousands of public discussion lists that you can subscribe to.

Blogger.com

www.blogger.com

A free blogging tool can be found at blogger.com. It is a very popular application that can get your blog up and running in minutes.

MyISPFinder

www.myispfinder.org

MyISPFinder will help you find and choose an ISP in your state.

Merchant Accounts

Here are some companies that specialize in merchant accounts for online merchants and are First Data Merchant Services (FDMS) compatible.

- **1st American Card Service**: 1stamericancardservice.com
- **Card Service International**: cardservice.com
- **Chase Merchant Services**: chasemerchantservices.com
- **Wells Fargo Merchant Services**: wellsfargo.com
- **First Bank**: fbol.com
- **Bank of Hawaii**: boh.com
- **Express Merchant Processing Solutions**: empsebiz.com
- **First Interstate Bank**: firstinterstatebank.com
- **Paymentech**: paymentech.com

Nolo

www.nolo.com

The Nolo website is a great resource for information on the different forms of business entities and how to form them.

PRWeb

www.prweb.com

Online news and press release distribution service.

Webmaster World

www.webmasterworld.com

News and discussions for web professionals.

Mailing List Resources

GOT Campaigner

Campaigner can help you grow your customer base, increase sales, create repeat customers, and measure the ROI (return on investment) of each direct emailing campaign.

Constant Contact

www.constantcontact.com

Do-It-Yourself email marketing service that will allow you to manage your email list and create email newsletters.

infoUSA Prospecting Lists

infoUSA is the premier provider of business and consumer mailing lists, sales leads, and databases. infoUSA, Inc. is the only company that compiles business and consumer data under one roof.

Financial Resources

Business Owners Idea Café

www.businessownersideacafe.com/financing/budget_calculator.html

A very simple, free budget calculator can be found at the Business Owners Idea Café.

Interest Rate Monitor

bankrate.com/brm/rate/cc_home.asp

Bank Rate Monitor lists lots of frequently updated information on which banks and credit card companies offer the best rates.

Unique Selling Position Worksheet

In Chapters 3, "Creating a Unique Selling Position," and 4, "Planning to Succeed," we discussed the elements of a unique selling position (USP) for your business. Now is the time to integrate those elements into a useful and effective USP for your eCommerce website.

The elements we will use are

- Shopper motivations to buy

- Meeting human needs

- The four Ps of a USP

- The three Cs of eCommerce

- The big 5 of online shopping

The object of this worksheet is to look at each of these elements and decide which of them, and which parts of them, will help define your USP, and then integrate them into an effective USP.

Shopper Motivations to Buy

Let's start with a shopper's motivation to buy. What shopper motivation are you targeting? List how your product or service will meet one, some, or all of these motivations to buy for your target customer.

- **Product or service motivator**: The need to satisfy with merchandise or service. This is the most common shopper motivation.

  _____

  _____

  _____

- **Information motivator**: The need to know. Are you selling any form of information? Information can be either a product or a service.

  _____

  _____

  _____

- **Entertainment motivator**: The need to be entertained. Perhaps your product or service has entertainment factors to it. For example, a DVD or CD would fill both the entertainment and product or service motivators.

  _____

  _____

  _____

- **Community**: The need to connect with other human beings. Perhaps you will have a community element to your product or service where customers may want to interact with each other for a fee.

  _____

  _____

  _____

Meeting Human Needs

Next, what human needs are you meeting with your product or service? List how your product or service will meet one, some, or all of these needs.

- **Physical needs**: Food, clothing, shelter

  _____

  _____

  _____

■ **Safety needs**: Protecting self, family, home

_____

_____

_____

■ **Belonging needs**: To be loved, have friends, be part of a family

_____

_____

_____

■ **Esteem needs**: Recognition and vanity

_____

_____

_____

The Four Ps of a USP

Next, which or the four Ps define your USP? List how your product or service will include one, some, or all of the Ps.

■ **Packaging**: Repackaging a common product or concept. For example, coffee (Starbucks), ice cream (Ben & Jerry's), popcorn (Orville Redenbacher), water (Dasani), and the iMac.

_____

_____

_____

■ **Positioning**: Selecting a niche. A good example is the Marines. They are looking for only a few good men. Another example is the Pepsi Generation. Can your product or service carve out a unique niche?

_____

_____

_____

■ **Pricing**: Lowest, highest, unique, value added. Where will you be on the pricing scale? Whatever it is, be prepared to defend the price you charge. If you are the lowest, why? If you are the highest, what added value do you provide?

_____

_____

_____

■ **Promotion**: Time of year, cultural event, or demographic. Perhaps you will focus on a specific time of year to sell your product or service: for example, holiday decorations at Christmas time or a tax service at tax time. Maybe you sell party supplies or Mother's Day gifts. Or perhaps you will sell to a specific demographic, such as teens, seniors, or an ethic group.

The Three Cs of eCommerce

Next, you must consider the three Cs of eCommerce and how they can be used to generate your USP. Write down how you would use these in offering your product or service.

■ **Content**: Selling products and services in a context relevant to your target audience. What kind of content will you have that will help sell your product aside from the copy that explains your product or service? Will you be a trusted expert describing the market that your product or service dwells within? Will you offer timely news, articles, or product and service reviews? How about online tools such as checklists, calculators, evaluators, or reality simulators? All of these are examples provide refreshable content that draws shoppers to your eCommerce site and could bring them back time and time again.

■ **Community**: Creating an online environment where visitors and customers can participate and interact with each other, such as discussion and message boards, chat rooms, electronic newsletters, and forms of personalization.

■ **Commerce**: The revenue-generating streams of your website. There is more than one way to make money from your site visitors. The first, of course, is through the sales of your products or services. But you can also generate revenue by selling advertising on your site, sponsorships, or joining another company's affiliate program, selling products or services that complement your offering.

_____

_____

_____

The Big Five of Online Shopping

Finally, you need to consider how your product or service offering meets the big five of online shopping. List how your product or service will meet each of these online shopping elements.

■ **Price**: What price will you sell at and why? This is very similar to the Price factor in the four Ps. You can use the same rationale here for your product or service. If the lowest, why? If the highest, why? If you're adding value, then what value? Will you guarantee lowest price? How?

_____

_____

_____

■ **Selection**: Will you offer a wide selection of products or services but not a deep one (books or music in all genres), or a focused selection but not wide (sci-fi books only)?

_____

_____

_____

■ **Convenience**: Ease of ordering. This includes company policies, live chat, and multiple ways to pay.

_____

_____

_____

■ **Service**: Will your company offer any warrantees, liberal return policies, or customer satisfaction guarantees?

_____

_____

_____

■ **Security**: Credit card and personal privacy guarantees. Besides these obvious security guarantees, your product or service might require additional guarantees such as jewelry appraisals or authentication guarantees on collectibles or antiques.

Integrating Your List and Establishing the USP

Now it's time to take the list that you've created and integrate the elements into one cohesive unique selling position. Look at the elements you have chosen that represent what the USP of your product or service is and how you plan to offer it to prospective customers.

By integrating your chosen elements you will have a useful and effective USP for your eCommerce website.

Here's an example.

Let's say your Yahoo! store sells Native American jewelry—in this case, authentic jewelry made by the Sioux nation.

■ The **motivation** of your target customer is the need to satisfy with merchandise.

■ The **human need** being met is the esteem need of recognition or vanity.

■ **Positioning** (selecting a jewelry niche market) and **pricing** (high end specialty jewelry) and perhaps **promotion** (a specific ethnic group such as the Sioux) are three of the four Ps.

■ Of the three Cs, **content** will be important, not only to describe the product but also the background of the tribe, the cultural uses of the jewelry, and how it is made.

■ As for the big 5, we've mentioned **price** (high-end and high-quality), a narrowly focused **selection** (not just Native American jewelry but Sioux jewelry), and **security** (the jewelry meets the Indian Arts and Crafts Act of 1990 as being authentic and a certificate is included for each piece) .

Here's another example. Suppose you have a Yahoo! store that offers a Serbian Travel Agency service.

■ The **motivation** of your target customer is the need to satisfy with a service, the need to know, and the need to connect with others of like interest.

- There are no direct **human needs** being met here.

- **Positioning** (selecting a travel destination niche market) and **pricing** (high-end, value-added travel packages and advice) and **promotion** (a specific ethnic group such as those traveling to Serbia) are three of the four Ps.

- Of the three Cs, **content** will be very important, not only to describe the product, but also to give background information and reviews on places to stay and things to see and do. **Community**, the ability to interact with others of similar interest and rate their experiences with the service, will also be important.

- As for the big 5, we've mentioned **price** (high-end, value-added travel packages), a narrowly focused **selection** (Serbian travel packages), **convenience** (Serbian information all in one place and advice on where to go and what do and see), and **service** (someone to call on for aid and advice when in Serbia).

These examples show how a well-integrated USP that is *built in to* your Yahoo! store will help your business compete, give shoppers a reason to buy from you, and act as a foundation for digital promotion strategy.

Index

J – K – L

jpg file formats, 132

keywords
 reports, 216
 searches
  market research, 31
  search engine
   optimization strategies,
   174-176, 180
 Store Editor, adding via,
  177-179

Lavasoft Ad-Aware
 anti-spyware software,
 94
Layout button (Store Editor),
 126
letterheads, 96
Link button (Store Editor),
 126
links (websites), search
 engine optimization
 strategies, 174, 181
List of Marketing Lists
 website, The, 243
LISTSERV list websites, 246
Liszt website, 166
live customer support,
 eCommerce, 47
loans, business plan
 development, 67
Look button (Store Editor),
 126
Lsoft website, 165-166, 246
lurking, 163

M

Macromedia Fireworks, 91
Mail Order/Telephone Order
 (MOTO), 209
mailing addresses (customer
 service), 46
mailing lists, 19, 246-247
Manage My Services control
 panel, 154

Manage My Services home
 page, 121-122
Manage Your Items link
 (Catalog Manager), 128,
 147
Manager button (Store
 Editor), 126
managing inventory
 developing procedures for,
  213-214
 Merchant Solutions,
  144-146
manual orders, processing,
 204
Manual Transaction
 Manager, processing
 orders, 204
Marines, marketing, 39
market research, 23, 31
Market Research Wizard
 website, 31
marketing
 Apple computers, 39
 blogs, 163, 166-167
 business associations, 162
 business plan development,
  67
 Delphi Forums website,
  164-166
 directories, registering with,
  173
 discussion lists, 163-166
 email, 191
  customer lists, 193-194
  GOT Campaigner, 194
  newsletters, 167-170
  opt-in email, 192-194
  signatures, 164
  spam, 192
 Four Ps of Marketing, 39-40
 Guerillas in the Mist article
  (MyEcommerceSuccess.
  com), 161
 iMac, 39
 Liszt website, 166
 Lsoft website, 165-166
 Marines, 39
 newsgroups, 163
 search engines, 172-174
 shipping boxes, 162

 shopping destination
  websites, registering with,
  195-196
 URLs, 162
 Yahoo! Groups website,
  163-165
Marketing Services (Yahoo!
 Merchant Solutions
 packages), 100
Marketing Strategies
 (business plans), 69
Marketing tools (Yahoo!
 Merchant Solutions
 packages), 100
Marketplace analyses
 (business plans), 69
marking orders, 208
McAfee AntiSpyware, 93
McAfee VirusScan, 93
Media Mail (USPS), 79
memory (computers), 89
merchandise
 acquisitions, business plan
  development, 66
 descriptions
  meta descriptions,
   178-180
  meta keywords, 174-179
  search engine
   optimization strategies,
   174-175, 180
 Four Ps of Marketing, 39
 home page, adding to, 136
 inventory levels, setting,
  146
 online stores, adding/
  editing
  Catalog Manager (Store
   Manager), 128-129
  Store Editor (Store
   Manager), 125-126, 130
  video example, 127
 selling, choosing to, 21
  business plan
   development, 65
  customer motivations,
   selling to, 22-23
  customer needs, selling to,
   24-29
  market research, 31
  versus services, 30

upgrading Merchant Solutions packages, 104

Upload button (Store Editor), 127, 132

Upload tool (Catalog Manager), 130

UPS (United Parcel Service), 79
  Online Tools, 143
  packages, tracking, 228-229

URLs (uniform resource locators)
  domain names, registering, 58-60
  marketing strategies, 162
  reports, 216

USP (Unique Selling Positions), developing
  advantages, determining, 37
  business image, 37
  competition
    differentiating from, 37-38
    tracking, 38
  consumers, determining reasons for usage, 37
  customer niches, 21
    belonging needs, selling to, 28
    esteem needs, selling to, 29
    motivations, selling to, 22-23
    physical needs, selling to, 24-25
    safety needs, selling to, 26-27
  Domino's Pizza example, 37
  Federal Express (FedEx) example, 36
  Four Ps of Marketing, 39-40
  WIIFM (What's in it for me?), 36-37
  worksheets, 249
    commerce, 253
    community, 252
    content, 252
    convenience, 253

customer needs, meeting, 250

customers' motivations to buy, 250
packaging, 251
positioning, 251
price, 253
pricing, 251
promotions, 252
security, 254
selection, 253
service, 253
USP development, incorporating in, 254-255

USPS (United States Postal Service)
  Express Mail, 78
  Media Mail, 79
  packages, tracking, 228
  Parcel Post, 79
  Priority Mail, 79
  websites, 79

V – W

variables page (Store Editor), 179
  accessing, 134
  Button Properties section, 135
  Colors and Typefaces section, 134
  Image Dimensions section, 134
  meta keywords, 177
  Page Layout section, 135
  Page Properties section, 135
  Store Properties section, 135

vendors, problem-solving strategies, 56

verification (addresses), 211

viruses, 93-94

VirusScan (McAfee), 93

Void Sale button (Order Manager), 207

voiding orders, 206-208

Wal-Mart, 58

warehouse space, business plan development, 66

web browsers, 92

Web Commerce Today website, 245

Web commerce websites, 246

Web connections, home/small office configurations, 98

Web Hosting (Yahoo! Merchant Solutions)
  advantages of, 107
  Dreamweaver, 107
  SiteBuilder, 107
  Store Editor
    comparison chart, 104-105
    switching to, 106

Web Position Gold website, 183

weblogs
  marketing strategies, 163, 166-167
  websites, 246
  Yahoo! 360, 167

Webmaster World website, 247

websites
  Barnes & Noble, 59
  contact us/about us pages, 118
  content, planning, 118
  data, organizing, 119
  design, Yahoo! Merchant Solutions packages, 101
  discounts, Yahoo! Merchant Solutions packages, 100
  home pages, 118
  item pages, 118
  links, 174, 181
  lurking, 163
  management, Yahoo! Merchant Solutions packages, 101
  materials, organizing, 119
  navigation menus, 118
  privacy policies, 118
  search engine optimization strategies
    links, 174, 181
    software, 183
    web resource, 184

Take Your Yahoo! Business to the Next Level!

ISBN: 0789735342
By Frank Fiore and Linh Tang
$24.99 USD
Available in June 2006!

Now that you've got your business up and running, make sure you have what it takes to make it a success! Frank Fiore and Linh Tang help you take your business to the next level with their follow-up book, *Succeeding at Your Yahoo! Business*. Discover how to customize your storefront so that it stands out from the crowd, and learn the keys to positioning, acquiring customers, accounting, marketing, and more!

Order your copy from www.quepublishing.com,
your favorite online retailer or your local bookstore!

Save big on essential small business services from Yahoo!

 **Save 25% for three months plus a waived setup fee on new Yahoo! web hosting and e-commerce accounts[1].**

Want to build a business website?

Utilize Yahoo!'s web hosting services to get your business in front of millions. You'll get a domain name, access to easy, free web building tools, business email accounts, and 24 hour toll-free customer support!

Want to sell online?

Build an e-commerce site with Yahoo! Merchant Solutions. Choose the package that best fits your needs, and begin ringing up your online sales. This special offer can save you almost $275[2]!

Sign up now at http://smallbusiness.yahoo.com/LaunchingYourYahooBusiness and receive 25% off web hosting or e-commerce services for 3 months, plus we'll waive the setup fee! Enter code YAHOONOW at signup.

 **Drive traffic to your web site. Get a $50 credit[3] on Yahoo!® Sponsored Search.**

Instead of looking for customers, what if they found you? Yahoo!® Sponsored Search lists your site in search results across the Web, so you connect with customers who are looking for what you have to offer.

Get your $50 credit by visiting http://sponsoredsearch.yahoo.com/smartonline or for Fast Track® assisted sign up service, call 800-313-1392 and mention promo code US1846B.